THE CYPRUS PROBLEM

THE CYPRUS PROBLEM

WHAT EVERYONE NEEDS TO KNOW

JAMES KER-LINDSAY

OXFORD
UNIVERSITY PRESS

OXFORD
UNIVERSITY PRESS

Oxford University Press
Oxford University Press, Inc., publishes works that further
Oxford University's objective of excellence
in research, scholarship, and education.

Oxford   New York
Auckland   Cape Town   Dar es Salaam   Hong Kong   Karachi
Kuala Lumpur   Madrid   Melbourne   Mexico City   Nairobi
New Delhi   Shanghai   Taipei   Toronto

With offices in
Argentina   Austria   Brazil   Chile   Czech Republic   France   Greece
Guatemala   Hungary   Italy   Japan   Poland   Portugal   Singapore
South Korea   Switzerland   Thailand   Turkey   Ukraine   Vietnam

Copyright © 2011 by James Ker-Lindsay

Published by Oxford University Press, Inc.
198 Madison Avenue, New York, New York 10016

www.oup.com

Oxford is a registered trademark of Oxford University Press

Library of Congress Cataloging-in-Publication Data
Ker-Lindsay, James, 1972–
The Cyprus problem : what everyone needs to know / James Ker-Lindsay.
    p.   cm.
Includes bibliographical references and index.
ISBN 978-0-19-975715-2 (pbk. : alk. paper)—ISBN 978-0-19-975716-9 (hbk. : alk. paper)
1. Cyprus—Ethnic relations   2. Greeks—Cyprus—History.
3. Turks—Cyprus—History.   4. Ethnic conflict—Cyprus—History.
5. Cyprus—Politics and government.   6. Peace-building—
Cyprus—History.   7. United Nations—Peacekeeping
forces—Cyprus—History.   8. Cyprus—History.
9. Cyprus—Social conditions.   I. Title.
DS54.4.K47 2011
956.9304—dc22   2010032099

Printed in the United States of America
on acid-free paper

CONTENTS

ACKNOWLEDGMENTS

My first debt of gratitude is to everyone who took the time to help me learn about Cyprus and its 'problem' over the past two decades. This book is a product of countless conversations and interviews with political figures, diplomats, journalists, academics, as well as ordinary Cypriots from all communities and walks of life.

Thanks also go to all my colleagues, both at LSEE-Research on South East Europe at the London School of Economics for providing such a friendly, interesting, and fun environment in which to work and at South East European Studies at Oxford (SEESOX), St Antony's College, Oxford University for so kindly 'adopting' me a number of years ago. It has always meant more to me than they realise.

My deepest appreciation goes to the team at Oxford University Press—Tim Bent, Dayne Poshusta, Tisse Takagi, Mally Anderson, Norma McLemore, and Michael O'Connor—for their comments, help, and advice, and to Tim Judah, the author of the book on Kosovo in this same series, for putting me in touch with the press in the first place. I would also like to say a special thank you to my dear friends Hubert

Faustmann, Fiona Mullen, Max Gevers, and Robert Holland for their invaluable contributions to the development of this book.

As ever, my greatest thanks go to Biljana. This book is dedicated to our son, John Milan.

INTRODUCTION

For almost sixty years, the small Mediterranean island of Cyprus has been a regular feature in the news. From the anti-colonial uprising against British rule in the 1950s through the emergence of fighting between the Greek and Turkish Cypriot communities in the 1960s, the Turkish invasion of the island in the 1970s, and the subsequent thirty-year effort by the United Nations to reunite the island, Cyprus has received a disproportionate degree of international attention.

For the most part, this interest has little to do with the intrinsic importance of the island itself. It has no significant mineral wealth. Nor is it a vital transit route to the Middle East, as it once was. Instead, the island's significance is due to wider geopolitical factors. Throughout the Cold War, conflict on the island had the potential to ignite an armed confrontation between NATO allies Greece and Turkey. More recently, the division of the island has played a central role in Turkey's aspirations to join the European Union. This is significant inasmuch as the relationship between the EU and Turkey could well determine how the union evolves as a regional body and what sort of ties it will have with its neighbours and the wider world. However, this is not the whole story. The attention devoted to the island is also a result of the level of notoriety it has achieved over the years. The Cyprus Problem (or the Cyprus issue), as it is often called, has become a byword for an intractable international conflict. No matter how much effort was exerted by various UN secretaries-general—to date, six have devoted time to the issue—it appears to be stubbornly immune to all peacemaking initiatives. Indeed, many eminent diplomats, including Richard Holbrooke, the architect of the Dayton Accords, which contributed to ending the bloody civil war in Bosnia, have tried, and failed, to find a solution to the Cyprus Problem, thus earning the island the title the 'diplomats' graveyard'. Others take a more cynical view, believing that the Cypriots have little inclination to reach a solution as they actually rather enjoy the international attention they receive. As George Mikes, a Hungarian wit, once famously, if rather unfairly, put it, 'Realizing they will never be a world power, the Cypriots have decided to settle for being a world nuisance'.

The high level of interest in the island is also the result of familiarity. Despite its division, the island of Cyprus is a popular holiday destination. Every year, tens of thousands of British, German, Russian, and Scandinavian tourists make their way to the island to enjoy its beaches, restaurants, and nightlife. Many have liked it so much that they have retired to the island. At the same time, Greek and Turkish Cypriots have established large expatriate communities in Europe, North America, Australia, and Africa.

And yet, for all of this, the Cyprus Problem remains extremely confusing for most outsiders. Though the foundation of the conflict between the Greek and Turkish Cypriot communities is a relatively straightforward dispute between two ethnic groups over power and geography, the details can be fiendishly complex. Seemingly trivial points take on major importance. Matters are not helped by the fact that the two sides have radically differing views on the origins of the conflict and how it should be resolved. Moreover, terms such as 'bizonality', 'bicommunality', 'federalism', and 'political equality' have very specific meanings depending on which side of the Green Line—the buffer zone dividing the two communities—you are on. Indeed, even within the two communities, there are stark differences of opinion on key questions. For all these reasons, it is often extremely difficult for outsiders to come to grips with Cyprus. This book aims to address that problem. By answering the most commonly asked questions posed by people trying to understand the many diverse and confusing aspects of the Cyprus Problem, this work will trace the history of the island and examine the issues at stake. It will also try to explain why a solution has been so hard to find and analyse a number of factors that could shape the future of the island, its two main communities, and the wider region.

STRUCTURE OF THE BOOK

As is often the case in conflicts, the past plays a significant role in shaping the positions of the two sides. The first chapter therefore explores a range of historical questions that are essential to understand in order to build a rounded and balanced picture of the Cyprus problem. The chapter begins by detailing the origins of the Greek and Turkish Cypriot communities and the other indigenous communities that live on the island (Maronites, Latins, Armenians, and Gypsies). Then it traces Cypriot history by addressing a range of key questions and queries that relate to various facets of the contemporary

Cyprus issue. The chapter concludes by examining the path to independence in 1960 and by explaining the complex constitutional provisions and international treaties that were put in place to safeguard the new state.

The second and third chapters examine the problems that emerged between the Greek and Turkish Cypriot communities after independence in 1960. Chapter 2 looks at the attitudes of the two sides towards the new state and explains the constitutional problems that emerged before analysing the start of intercommunal fighting in 1963 and the origins of the UN presence on the island. Chapter 3 explores the invasion and the division of the island in 1974 and the subsequent efforts by the UN and the international community to reunite Cyprus.

The fourth chapter provides a guide to the range of issues that divide the two communities. It begins with an analysis of what is meant by a 'bizonal, bicommunal federation' as the agreed basis for reunification, and shows how the two sides have very different conceptions of the term. It then explains the structure of the new state and its international legal personality before addressing the key concerns of the two sides over questions such as property, refugee returns, and the repatriation of settlers. It concludes by examining the key issues concerning security, such as the demilitarisation of the island and the differences over the role of guarantees in any settlement.

The fifth and last chapter explores a number of general questions that often arise when people start to learn about Cyprus, framing these in the context of current and future efforts to resolve the Cyprus Problem. It looks at the international actors and factors shaping the settlement process, such as the role of the UN and the European Union, and the roles played by Britain, Greece, and Turkey. Finally, it analyses the underlying wishes of the two communities, the exact type of settlement the two communities want, and whether partition really is the 'best' solution—as many observers increasingly suggest.

A NOTE ON LANGUAGE AND TERMINOLOGY

Writing about any conflict is rarely easy. The Cyprus Problem is no different. Every comment or explanation is analysed for bias and every turn of phrase carefully parsed for prejudice. Likewise, what is left out is as often cause for criticism as the information included. The guiding spirit behind this book is to serve readers who want to quickly familiarise themselves with the history of the island's political problems and to understand the key issues shaping the search for a solution, not to benefit one side over another. As a concise account of the Cyprus Problem, the book has necessarily had to adopt a judicious approach to detail, dramatically condensing some periods and omitting arcane information that is not needed by someone just starting to explore the complexity of the Cyprus issue.

Another difficult issue for anyone dealing with Cyprus is terminology. The terms and phrase one uses can betray where one stands on aspects of the Cyprus problem. This book tries to adopt the standard usage of terms. The Republic of Cyprus, as officially internationally recognised, covers the whole of the island. However, in reality, its area of effective administration covers only the southern two-thirds of it. The remaining third—the north—is composed of the self-proclaimed Turkish Republic of Northern Cyprus (TRNC), which is recognised only by Turkey. In terms of main protagonists, the official usage is adopted. Thus the leader of the Greek Cypriots is the president of the Republic of Cyprus, whereas the president of the TRNC is generally recognised as the leader of the Turkish Cypriot community.

Likewise, the term 'invasion' is often disputed. While it has always been used by Greek Cypriots, many Turkish Cypriots prefer to use the word 'intervention' or, even more benignly, 'peace operation'. Recently, however, use of the word 'invasion' has become less politically sensitive (perhaps as a result of the invasion of Iraq). Simply put, the Turkish military operations in 1974 were quite clearly invasions, regardless of whether one feels that they were justified.

Another contentious issue is place names. In many cases, a city or town will have both Greek and Turkish names that are equally recognised and accepted, such as Lefkosia/Lefkosa, Kyreneia/Girne and Pafos/Baf. However, in the north of the island, the Turkish Cypriot authorities have changed the names of many villages previously inhabited by Greek Cypriots. To avoid confusion, this book adopts the names as most usually used or recognised in English: Nicosia, Kyrenia, and Paphos, in the cases above.

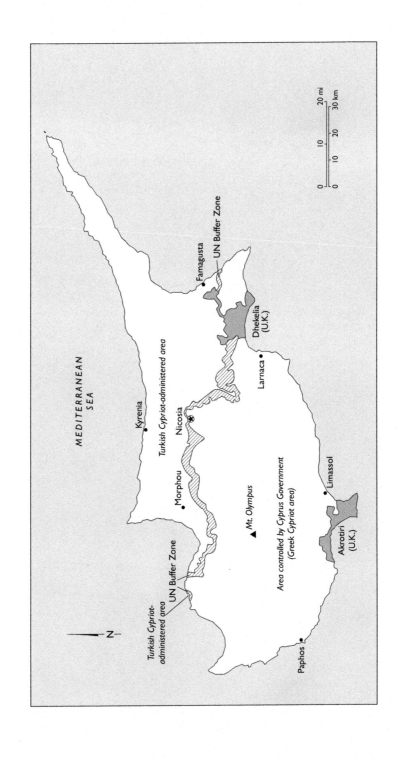

MEDITERRANEAN
SEA

Kyrenia

Morphou

Turkish Cypriot-administered area

UN Buffer Zone

Turkish Cypriot-
administered area

N

▲ Mt. Olympus

Nicosia

Famagusta

UN Buffer Zone

Dhekelia
(U.K.)

Larnaca

Area controlled by Cyprus Government
(Greek Cypriot area)

Limassol

Akrotiri
(U.K.)

Paphos

0   10   20 mi
0   10   20   30 km

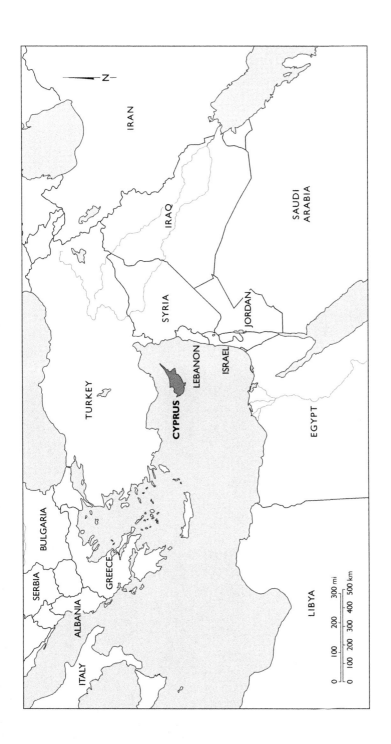

THE CYPRUS PROBLEM

1
SOCIAL AND HISTORICAL BACKGROUND

WHAT AND WHERE IS CYPRUS?

The island of Cyprus lies at the farthest eastern end of the Mediterranean Sea at the crossroads between Europe, Africa, and Asia. Its nearest neighbour, Turkey, lies approximately 50 miles north of the island. Next closest, lying 70 miles to the east, are Syria and Lebanon. Egypt is 240 miles south. Travelling westwards, the nearest Greek island, Castellorizo, is 170 miles away, with the Greek mainland an additional 330 miles away from Cyprus. At its extremes, the island is 150 miles long from east to west, and 100 miles wide from north to south. Its total land area is 3,572 square miles (9,251 square kilometres). It is the third-largest island in the Mediterranean, after Sardinia and Sicily. Were Cyprus a U.S. state, it would be number 48 in size—falling between Connecticut and Delaware.

The island is home to two mountain ranges—the Troodos, to the west, and Kyrenia (Pentydactylos), which runs along the north coast of the island. These are divided by a central plain, the Mesaoria, which is the centre of the island's agricultural activity. The coastline is central to the tourist industry, a key income generator for the economy, and to business services. Nicosia is the capital of the island and the largest city.

The other main urban areas are Limassol, Famagusta, Larnaca, Morphou, and Kyrenia. There is some dispute over the origin of the island's name. A commonly accepted view is that Cyprus takes is name from *cuprum*, the Latin word for copper. However, it has also been suggested that the name is far older, deriving from the word for copper used by the Eteocypriots, the pre-Hellenic indigenous inhabitants of the island.

WHO ARE THE GREEK CYPRIOTS?

The Greek Cypriots are the largest ethnic group in Cyprus. At the time of independence in 1960, when the last official census of the island's population was carried out, there were 441,568 Greek Cypriots, accounting for 78 percent of the island's inhabitants. In 2008, the total population of the areas under control of the government stood at 796,900, according to official statistical data. However, this figure includes religious minorities and foreigners, who would account for 15 percent to 20 percent of this total. Accurate population figures taking account of the Turkish Cypriots, the other main community, do not exist. In lieu of accurate new data, the figure of 78 percent is still widely cited as the approximate size of the Greek Cypriot community in relation to the island's population as a whole.

The first Greek community on the island is generally believed to have been formed by Achaean and Mycenaean Greek settlers who arrived on the island during the middle Bronze Age thirty-five hundred to four thousand years ago. There they lived alongside the Eteocypriots, the indigenous inhabitants, and, later, the Phoenicians, who established settlements in the ninth century BC. In 526 BC, Cyprus was conquered by the Persians, who retained control until 333 BC, when it was conquered by Alexander the Great. Following his death, Cyprus became part of Ptolemaic Egypt. During this era, Cyprus was integrated into the wider Hellenic world. Its most famous son from this period is Zeno of Citium, the founder of the Stoic school of philosophy. In 58 BC, Cyprus came under Roman control. When the Roman Empire split in the fourth century AD, the island became a part of the Eastern province—which eventually became better known as the Greek-speaking Byzantine Empire. Despite periods of Arab domination following the rise of Islam, the island remained under Byzantine rule until the end of the twelfth century.

It is obvious that Cyprus has had strong links with the wider Hellenic world for much of its history. But in contemporary terms it is difficult to precisely define a Greek Cypriot. Even within the Greek Cypriot community, opinion is divided on the question of identity. At one end of the scale are those Greek Cypriots who see themselves as Greek first and foremost, placing little if any emphasis on a Cypriot identity. They are Greeks who happen to live on the island of Cyprus, just as 'Cretans' are accepted as Greeks who happen to live in Crete and 'Athenians' are Greeks who live in Athens. Historical circumstances may have denied them a place in the Greek state, but they are no less Greeks than anyone living within Greece. At the other end of the spectrum are those who prefer to stress their Cypriot identity. They reject any particular emphasis on their 'Greekness', although few deny it altogether, opting instead to see themselves as culturally and historically tied to the island of Cyprus above all else. Their allegiance is to Cyprus. Greece is a distant and foreign land. As one might expect, most Greek Cypriots fall between the two positions. They recognise that they have a Greek identity but see themselves as clearly distinct from the Greeks from Greece. They have a specifically Cypriot character and a distinct Cypriot dialect, and they feel a strong allegiance to their island even though they may still feel a bond, however strong or weak, with Greece.

In many areas, close links do exist. For example, many Greek Cypriots study at Greek universities, and most support the Greek football team when it plays in international competitions. Likewise, many of the television shows and leading music artists that Cypriots watch and listen to are Greek, although there are notable cases of Cypriots achieving stardom in Greece.

Not unsurprisingly, this ambiguous relationship between Greece and Cyprus, or between the Greeks and Greek Cypriots, confuses outsiders. Even foreigners who have lived on the island for many years find it hard to decipher. One of the most common comments one hears concerns the prevalence of the Greek flag. (It should be noted that this has declined significantly since 2004. Now, usually EU flags fly alongside the Cypriot flag on public buildings.) Outsiders often cannot understand why Cyprus, as an independent state, would fly the flag of another country. Again, one has to read it in the context of the complex relationship that exists between Greek Cypriots and Greece. In many ways, it would be better to see it not as a symbol of the Greek state but as a symbol of the wider Greek nation—of which the Greeks living in Greece and the Greek Cypriots might be thought of as two parts. It is a flag of ethnic, not political, unity. While there are linguistic, cultural, and religious ties between Greece and the Greek Cypriots, the reality is that very few Greek Cypriots feel any sort of allegiance to the Greek state as such. All this may, of course, sound rather contradictory. But identity issues are often that way.

Related to this is the common Turkish Cypriot assertion that the Greek Cypriots are beholden to Greece. Some even argue that Greek Cypriots still wish to pursue some sort of political union with Greece (*enosis*, of which I'll say more later on). This is not true. Were a referendum held tomorrow, it is doubtful that even 5 percent of Greek Cypriots would vote in favour of unification. Very few Greek Cypriots want to give up their independence to become a distant province of Greece. At one time, such an idea was alluring, but no more. Tied to this is another frequent Turkish Cypriot accusation that Greece controls the Greek Cypriots. Again, this has no basis in reality. The Greek government has no formal power to determine the decisions of the Greek Cypriots, and there is no evidence to suggest that it tries to exercise control over the Greek Cypriots. Indeed, if it were to do so, especially on domestic issues, it would be swiftly rebuffed by the Greek Cypriot political leadership and by the wider Greek Cypriot community. Even on the Cyprus issue, since 1974 the universally accepted principle is that, 'Nicosia decides, and Athens follows'.

WHO ARE THE TURKISH CYPRIOTS?

Compared to the Greek Cypriots, the Turkish Cypriot community is considerably smaller and has relatively more recent origins. At the time of independence, there were 103,822 Turkish Cypriots. This meant that they amounted to 18 percent of the total population of the island. Again, without new and reliable data, a more accurate contemporary assessment of the relative size of the community cannot be made, and thus the 18 percent figure is still generally used in discussions on the Cyprus issue.

The first members of the community arrived on the island following the Ottoman conquest of the island in 1571. In the centuries that followed, many more arrived. Their numbers were also bolstered by Greek Cypriots who converted to Islam to gain social and financial benefits (Christians were more heavily taxed), thereby becoming members of the Turkish Cypriot community. This leads many Greek Cypriots to feel that the Turkish Cypriots have less right to be on the island than their community. While the Greek Cypriots do indeed have a longer presence on the island, Turkish Cypriots have nevertheless been in Cyprus for almost 450 years. By all accounts, Cyprus is as much their home now as it is the home of the Greek Cypriots.

As with the Greek Cypriots, there are á range of views within the Turkish Cypriot community as to self-identity. Some Turkish Cypriots regard themselves as Turks living in Cyprus. Others see themselves as primarily Cypriot. Again, the majority view themselves as falling somewhere between the two positions. The picture is also confused by the arrival of large numbers of settlers from mainland Turkey since 1974. At first, this did not have too serious an effect. By and large, the new arrivals integrated well and readily adapted to Turkish Cypriot customs and ways. (Turkish Cypriots tend to be much less religious and more liberal than Anatolians.) Increasingly, though, this is changing. The pace of immigration—both in terms of those who are given citizenship by the Turkish Republic of Northern Cyprus (TRNC) and those who are simply temporary workers—is such that there is a real danger that the Turkish Cypriot community will be swamped and may eventually disappear altogether. This situation is exacerbated by the large numbers of Turkish Cypriots who have emigrated from the island over the past thirty years. While Greek Cypriot figures on the number of Turkish Cypriot settlers should be read with caution, many Turkish Cypriots express serious concerns about the implications of so many newly arrived mainland Turkish citizens for their community and identity.

Just as the Turkish Cypriots often accuse Greece of influencing the Greek Cypriots, so many Greek Cypriots accuse Turkey of having an undue influence over the Turkish Cypriots. Indeed, most Greek Cypriot politicians argue that the Turkish Cypriots have no power to negotiate a solution to the Cyprus issue. A settlement can come only from Turkey. But while there is little doubt that Turkey exercises a far greater degree of control over the north than Greece does over the south, things are not quite as straightforward as they might seem. On the one hand, it is hard to deny that Turkey wields significant power over the Turkish Cypriots. After all, it provides for their security with thirty thousand to forty thousand Turkish troops based on the island. Moreover, because of the economic isolation faced by the Turkish Cypriots as a result of the decision to unilaterally declare independence in 1983, Turkey supports their economy by providing an annual grant to the Turkish Cypriot administration.

Despite this, it would be wrong to assume that the Turkish Cypriots have no control over their own affairs. For many years, Rauf Denktash, the veteran Turkish Cypriot leader, wielded considerable influence in Turkey, so much that few politicians in Turkey would stand up to him. This changed with the election of the Justice and Development Party (AKP) in Turkey in November 2002. Since then, the Turkish Cypriots have showed a far greater willingness to reach a solution and, following Denktash's defeat in elections in 2005, allowed the moderate, pro-settlement administration under Mehmet Ali Talat—who was less charismatic than Denktash and did not have a power base in Turkey—to negotiate more freely than previous administrations. This begs the question of what will happen now that the Turkish Cypriots have once again elected a more hard-line leader, Dervis Eroglu. Will the Turkish government pressure him to reach a deal? It is hard to tell. All that can be said at this stage is that the relationship between Turkey and the Turkish Cypriots is more complicated than it might at first appear.

WHO ELSE LIVES ON THE ISLAND?

In addition to the Greek and Turkish Cypriot communities, there are three other constitutionally recognised groups living in Cyprus: the Maronites, Armenians, and Latins. There is also a small, but officially unrecognised, Gypsy community. Altogether, these groups made up the remaining 4 percent of the population, after the Greek and Turkish Cypriots, at the time of independence. Under the 1960 constitution, they are formally recognised as religious minorities rather than as 'communities', and are each entitled to send one member to the House of Representatives (the Cypriot parliament), who may vote on matters directly affecting their communities. To ensure that they would not be prevented from having a full say in the political process, all three religious groups were also asked to decide which of the two communities they wished to be a part of for participating in presidential and parliamentary elections. All three opted to be linked with the Greek Cypriot community.

The largest of the three groups, with a population of about six thousand, are the Maronites, who began immigrating to the island from Lebanon and Syria more than a thousand years ago. They retain their close religious links with the Maronite Church in Lebanon, a religious group that is in communion with the Catholic Church but retains many of its own rites and hierarchy. (For example, the Maronite patriarch is a cardinal in the Roman Catholic Church.) Until 1974, the Maronite community lived mostly in a few villages near Cape Kormakiti, in the northwestern part of the island, where they continued to speak the old Maronite dialect of Arabic. However, after 1974 most were forced to move to the south. In the years since then, they have become increasingly integrated into the Greek Cypriot community, and their separate traditions and language are now dying out.

The Armenians are thought to number approximately four thousand. Like the Maronites, they have a long-established history on Cyprus. There are records of Armenians serving with the Byzantine army on the island before the tenth century. However, there have also been several waves of Armenian immigration into Cyprus, including one at the start of the twentieth century, when many fled persecution within the Ottoman Empire. As a result of the division of the island in 1974, they, too, are almost exclusively based in the southern part of the island and are generally integrated within Greek Cypriot society. Traditionally, the Armenians have had little involvement in government and politics, often preferring to concentrate on commercial activity.

The smallest of the three religious communities, the Latins, number just a few hundred. They are the descendants of the Venetians, who ruled the island before the Ottoman conquest in 1571. They are Roman Catholic and can often be recognised by their Italian-sounding surnames. Like the Armenians, they have had little involvement in politics, perhaps because of the small size of their community.

The small community of Gypsies on the island lives in the north. No one knows their exact number, and they are rarely listed in any breakdown of the island's communities. In one of the later versions of the 2004 reunification plan (Annan Plan), they were recognised as an official community, but in the final version of the proposals there was no reference to them. In addition to the three constitutionally recognised religious minorities and the Gypsies, a number of other communities live on the island. A large number of Greek citizens live in the south. Most of these are Greek nationals who married Greek Cypriots or are Black Sea Greeks from the former Soviet Republic of Georgia who were given Greek citizenship after the Soviet Union collapsed in the 1990s, thereby entitling them to settle in Cyprus. They have formed communities in Paphos and Nicosia. And as said above, there has been large-scale immigration to the north by Turkish citizens. After Greeks and Turks, the next-largest community is that of British citizens who have set up homes on both sides of the Green Line. Though no reliable figures exist, it is generally accepted that they number around ten thousand, a figure that does not include the large number of Greek and Turkish Cypriots who hold British citizenship in addition to their Cypriot citizenship.

As a result of the political turmoil that emerged after the end of the Soviet Union and the wars in the Balkans and the Middle East, there are many Russians, Serbs, and Lebanese living on the island. There are also many thousands of foreign students and guest workers, mainly from Sri Lanka, Pakistan, Bangladesh, and the Philippines. After the island's accession to the European Union in May 2004, large numbers of workers came from central Europe, including Poles, Hungarians, and Slovaks. Also, by virtue of its location, Cyprus has become a hub for illegal immigrants seeking to enter the EU. Population figures suggest that Cyprus has the second-largest proportion of immigrants of any EU member state, exceeded only by Luxembourg. Like most other Western states, Cyprus in now home to a complex mixture of different nationalities and ethnic groups—not that this seems to have much bearing on the way in which the Greek and Turkish Cypriots tend to view one another.

WHO RULED CYPRUS IN THE PAST?

By virtue of its location at the far eastern end of the Mediterranean, Cyprus has always been regarded as a vital piece of strategic territory. As noted above, in ancient times it came under the rule of the Persians, Egyptians, Romans, Byzantines, and Arabs. In 1191, the island was conquered by King Richard the Lionheart on his way to the Holy Land as part of the Third Crusade. He quickly sold it on to the Knights Templar. Realising that they could not control the island's unruly inhabitants, they quickly changed their mind and asked for a refund. Richard agreed, but only after having found another buyer—Guy de Lusignan, the former king of Jerusalem. Thus began three hundred years of Frankish rule over what became the kingdom of Cyprus. In 1489, this period came to an end with the death of Caterina Cornaro, the last queen of Cyprus. Cyprus then passed to Venetian rule.

As one might expect, most of these conquerors have left some sort of mark on the island. For example, following the conversion of Sergius Paulus, the Roman proconsul of the island, by Saints Paul and Barnabus, Cyprus became the first territory in the world to be ruled by a Christian. Four centuries later, while under Byzantine rule, the Cypriot Orthodox Church was recognised as autocephalous—that is, independent from any of the patriarchates that governed other Orthodox territories. This gave the church, and its leader, important privileges. Arab rule also had its effect. An important Islamic religious shrine built around the final resting place of the aunt of the Prophet Muhammad can be found on the shores of the salt lake just outside of Larnaca. Three centuries of rule by the Crusader Lusignan dynasty can be seen in the architecture of the island. The most famous buildings from this era are Kolossi Castle, near Limassol, and the Church of Saint Nicholas, in Nicosia. Likewise, the Venetian rulers oversaw the construction of the mighty walls surrounding Nicosia and Famagusta, which still survive.

By the middle of the sixteenth century, the Ottoman Empire had conquered almost all of southeastern Europe and was in the process of securing full control over the eastern Mediterranean. In 1570, Sultan Selim II ordered the invasion of the island. Marching under the command of Mustafa Lala Pasha, the Ottoman forces conquered Nicosia after a brief siege. The sultan's army then marched eastwards and laid siege to the walled city of Famagusta. The city managed to hold out for almost a year before falling in August 1571. Although the Ottoman navy was subsequently beaten by Venetian and other Christian forces at the Battle of Lepanto, Venice was forced to accept the loss of Cyprus.

While Greek Cypriots often paint an extremely negative picture of Ottoman rule, the reality is rather more complex. Certainly there were hardships. After centuries of attention, Cyprus now became of marginal interest to the wider world. The island and its people suffered from punitive taxes and from neglect. Yet the island's new rulers also brought benefits. Most notably, the Ottoman conquest of the island may well have played a major role in ensuring the survival of Orthodox Christianity on the island. Under Lusignan and Venetian rule, the Catholic Church held primacy, and people were pressured to accept Rome's spiritual authority. (The most notable example of this was the Bulla Cypria issued by the Vatican in 1260. This document effectively gave control over appointments in the Orthodox Church to Catholic bishops on the island.) In contrast, the Muslim Ottomans took a much more benign view towards the Orthodox Church. As long as the people paid their taxes and did not rebel, the new rulers were happy to let them continue in their faith. Indeed, as happened elsewhere in the empire, the Church in Cyprus was co-opted into the running of the state, acting as the main link between the sultan and his Christian peoples. This meant that in addition to being the head of the church, the archbishop also assumed the title of ethnarch—leader of the Greek Cypriot people.

As for the relations between the Greek Cypriots and the newly emerging Turkish Cypriot community, on the whole there appeared to be relatively few problems between the two peoples for most of the Ottoman period and until the latter stages of British rule. However, this should not be misconstrued to mean that relations between the two were without tensions. Partly for political reasons, to show that Greek and Turkish Cypriots can get along, and partly because they seem to want to believe it, Greek Cypriots often paint a far rosier picture of the relationship than was the case. While some Greek and Turkish Cypriots may have formed friendships, on the whole the two communities did not mix. Many villages were made up of one group or the other. Where they did live in the same town or village, they lived in different areas and had little direct contact in day-to-day life. Intermarriage was very rare.

WHEN AND WHY DID CYPRUS COME UNDER BRITISH CONTROL?

By the late nineteenth century, the Ottoman Empire was in steep decline. Following the formation of the Greek state in the first half of the nineteenth century, it faced growing pressure for independence from its other Balkan subjects. At the same time, it came under increasing threat from Russia, which sought access to the Mediterranean from the Black Sea. This led to several major wars between Constantinople and Moscow, including the Crimean War (1853–56) and the Russo-Turkish War (1877–78).

After the latter war, during which the Ottoman Empire lost several eastern provinces, the European powers gathered for the Congress of Berlin. There the map of the Balkans was redrawn. With Russian support, Serbia, Montenegro, and Romania all became independent states. However, in an attempt to prevent further Russian aggression, Constantinople entered into an agreement with London to allow Britain to occupy and administer Cyprus. This agreement, known as the Cyprus Convention, was purely strategic in nature. In return for control of the island, London promised that it would help repel any future Russian attack on the Ottoman Empire's eastern provinces. For Britain, the convention was extremely beneficial geopolitically. Cyprus provided a useful base for ships travelling through the Suez Canal to India, Britain's most important colonial possession. Crucially, the agreement was only temporary. It stipulated that if Moscow returned the territories captured during the 1877–78 Russo-Turkish War, Britain would hand back Cyprus to full Ottoman rule.

WHAT WERE ENOSIS AND THE MEGALI IDEA?

Although the arrangement between London and Constantinople did not mark a formal end to Ottoman sovereignty over Cyprus, the transfer was nevertheless welcomed by the Greek-speaking Orthodox Christians who made up the majority of the population. They hoped that the transfer of administration would pave the way for the island to be united with Greece—an aspiration known as "enosis." At the time, these calls for enosis were not just limited to Cyprus. Instead, Cyprus was part of a wider political movement that sought to liberate and unify all Greeks living under Ottoman rule—whether in Macedonia, Asia Minor, the Black Sea, or Cyprus—in what many undoubtedly hoped would be a reconstructed Byzantium based in Constantinople. This overarching political ambition was known as the *Megali Idea* (great idea).

The Greek Cypriot belief that that enosis might occur was shaped in part by the important role Britain played in establishing the Greek state fifty years earlier. It was also seemingly encouraged by statements made in support of the idea by prominent British philhellenes such as William Gladstone, the leader of the Liberal Party. Despite making representations to the new British governor, Sir Garnett Wolseley, the Greek Cypriots were to be bitterly disappointed. Although London quickly realised that Cyprus actually had very little strategic value, largely because it did not have a deep-water harbour and because British troops could be garrisoned in Egypt, the British government made clear that it would not break its agreement with the Ottoman sultan and cede the island to Greece. Under British rule, enosis would not take place, and the *Megali Idea* would remain unrealised.

WHAT WAS BRITISH RULE LIKE?

While Britain made clear that it had no intention of relinquishing control of Cyprus, it did take steps to improve life for the islanders. For a start, it undertook a number of major infrastructure projects. At the same time, important political reforms were instituted that laid the foundations for democracy in Cyprus. For example, elections were held for new bodies, such as the Legislative Council, that had some influence on local and Cyprus-wide administration. At the same time, the British authorities decided not to exercise direct control over the educational system, allowing Greek- and Turkish-language schools to exist. Also, Greek- and Turkish-language newspapers began to emerge. However, there was another side to the arrangement. Under the terms of the Cyprus Convention, Britain had to pay a fixed annual sum to the Ottoman authorities. This was raised by taxation from the Cypriots themselves, who were also forced to pay for the costs of British administration. This 'tribute' hindered the island's economic development and contributed to resentment towards British rule.

Following the Ottoman Empire's decision to side with Germany at the start of the First World War, Britain's relationship with Cyprus changed dramatically. London annexed the island. In 1915, the following year, in a bid to induce Greece to join the war, London came close to granting the Greek Cypriots their wish and offered the island to Athens. Though the proposal was supported by Eleftherios Venizelos, the Greek prime minister, it was rejected by the Greek king, Constantine I, who was determined to keep Greece out of the war. In the decade that followed, Britain strengthened its control over Cyprus. In 1923, under the terms of the Treaty of Lausanne, the new Republic of Turkey, the successor to the Ottoman Empire, formally relinquished its claims to the island and called on Turkish Cypriots to leave the island and settle in Turkey. Few heeded the call. Appalled at living conditions in Anatolia at the time and effectively prevented from leaving

Cyprus by a largely unaffordable departure levy imposed by the British authorities, who did not want them to leave, most stayed where they were. On 10 March 1925, Britain formally declared Cyprus a Crown colony.

The removal of these last vestiges of formal Ottoman or Turkish sovereignty over the island led to renewed calls for enosis from the Greek Cypriots. But Britain continued to reject this idea, further angering the Greek Cypriot community. In 1931, Greek Cypriot frustrations reached the boiling point. Violent riots broke out, and the headquarters of the British administration on the island, the Government House, was burned down. The colonial authorities responded with measures designed to prevent similar incidents. These included a ban on flying the Greek flag, the prohibition of political parties, and increased censorship of the press. While these certainly limited public expressions of support for enosis, it did little to dampen pro-union sentiment. And while nationalist activity was put on hold during the Second World War, during which time the Greek Cypriots expressed loyalty to the British Empire in the hope that this would later be rewarded, as soon as the conflict came to an end there were renewed calls for Cyprus to unite with Greece. London, although now willing to examine the possibilities for some form of self-rule, nevertheless remained adamant that it would not relinquish its sovereignty over the island.

On 15 January 1950, the Ethnarchy Council, the Church-led supreme leadership of the Greek Cypriot community, held an islandwide unofficial referendum on the question of enosis. The result was near-unanimous support for enosis: about 96 percent of participating Greek Cypriots wished to see Cyprus and Greece unite.

WHO WAS ARCHBISHOP MAKARIOS?

At this time, the two most important figures in modern Cypriot history emerged. The first, Archbishop Makarios III, was born Michael Mouskos in 1913 to a poor family in a small village near Paphos, in the west of the island. He entered the priesthood at the age of 13 and, after studying in Greece, was awarded a scholarship in the United States. However, his studies there were cut short when he was elected bishop of Kition, taking the name Makarios. Just two years later, in 1950, Makarios was elected archbishop of Cyprus at age 37. Over the next decade, he played a central part in efforts to end British rule over the island, and when Cyprus became independent in 1960 he was elected as the first president of the new state. He held this post until his death in August 1977, despite several assassination attempts and the coup d'etat in 1974.

As one might expect, opinion about Makarios is sharply divided. Turkish Cypriots hold him responsible for bringing down the post-independence constitutional order and forcing them out of the government. Among Greek Cypriots, many fervently believe that for all his mistakes he ultimately sought the best for the Greek Cypriot people. Others, however, regard him as a traitor for eventually abandoning the dream of enosis. Internationally, he also provoked strong reactions. Christopher Hitchens, the author and journalist famed for his antireligious diatribes, called him the only priest he ever liked. Western leaders widely mistrusted him. His flirtations with the Soviet Union at the height of the Cold War, an effort to limit NATO influence on the island, and his key role in the nonaligned movement led many to view him as the Castro of the Mediterranean. As for Makarios the person, very little is known. He left no diaries or memoires. Even those close to him say that they rarely knew what he was thinking.

WHO IS RAUF DENKTASH?

The second major figure to emerge in the 1950s was Rauf Denktash. Born in Paphos in 1924, he qualified as a lawyer in Britain before returning to Cyprus. (This is actually a surprisingly common background for Cypriot figures—Presidents Kyprianou, Clerides, and Papadopoulos were also British-trained lawyers.) During the anticolonial uprising he led a double life, serving as a prosecutor for the British authorities and leading Turkish Cypriot resistance to enosis. Following independence, he became the president of the Turkish Cypriot communal chamber but continued his underground activities. After the outbreak of clashes in 1963, the Greek Cypriot–led government banned him from the island, arguing that he was a leader of the armed resistance. However, he returned to the island in 1968 and eventually replaced Dr. Fazil Kuchuk, the first vice president of Cyprus, as leader of the Turkish Cypriots. Following the Turkish invasion in 1974, his position became even stronger, and he was the key protagonist behind the Turkish Cypriot decision to declare independence, in 1983. He was subsequently elected as president of the 'Turkish Republic of Northern Cyprus', a post he held until 2005, when he was voted out of office. Despite his age, he remains active in politics and continues to write and speak on the Cyprus Problem.

Like Makarios, Denktash stirs up considerable emotions. To many Greek Cypriots, he is a hate figure and is seen as responsible for the division of the island. Even among Turkish Cypriots, the verdict is ambiguous. Although most recognise the important role he played in protecting their community, many also argue that by impetuously declaring independence he is the cause of their isolation. In terms of personality, he is known for his intelligence, wit, and, above all, stubbornness. Indeed, he seems to revel in his intransigence. One particularly memorable example of this came in the late 1990s when the British foreign secretary, Malcolm Rifkind, was reported to have tried to use reverse psychology to shame him into taking a moderate position on reunification talks. Asking the Turkish Cypriot leader how he would feel if history marked him down as the man who had failed to reunite Cyprus, Denktash simply replied that he felt that this would probably be a fair assessment.

WHAT WAS THE EOKA CAMPAIGN, AND HOW DID IT DEVELOP?

EOKA—the National Organisation of Cypriot Fighters—was the Greek Cypriot militia formed to end British rule in Cyprus and bring about the island's union with Greece. (Crucially, and unlike anticolonial movements elsewhere in the world, it did not fight for independence.) At the same time that the Greek Cypriots were becoming more active in their pursuit of enosis, the Greek government started to take more interest in the future of the island. This marked a departure from the position of previous governments, which had wished to avoid antagonising Britain—a key political and economic benefactor. However, the emergence of the United States as the preeminent patron of Greece and Turkey in the late 1940s changed the situation. In 1953, the Greek prime minister, Field Marshal Alexandros Papagos, decided to raise the issue of Cyprus during a meeting with Sir Anthony Eden, the British foreign secretary. Eden declined to discuss the matter. Outraged at this response, Papagos now adopted a much more hard-line stance. On 3 May 1954, he announced that Greece would take the matter to the United Nations, but the United Kingdom successfully argued that the matter was an internal issue and not a matter for the UN. The General

Assembly then decided not to deal with the Cyprus issue for the time being.

With the diplomatic and political avenues seemingly closed, Makarios authorised George Grivas, a Cypriot-born retired colonel of the Greek Army, to put together plans for an armed uprising to end British rule in Cyprus and unite the island with Greece. Despite rumours that a Greek Cypriot militia was being formed and weapons stockpiled, the British authorities apparently did not take the threat seriously. Indeed, it was not until January 1955, when a small Greek fishing boat boarded by the British Navy was found to be carrying a considerable quantity of weapons, that the true level of the threat became apparent. However, this discovery was made too late to stop the preparations for the rebellion. On 1 April 1955, a series of bombs exploded at administrative buildings around the island, marking the start of the EOKA uprising.

HOW DID THE TURKISH CYPRIOTS RESPOND TO THE EOKA REBELLION?

Despite its goal of achieving enosis, the EOKA leadership at first attempted to take a conciliatory line with the Turkish Cypriot community. In July 1955, just a few months after the start of the fighting, the organisation issued a Turkish-language pamphlet explaining its position and clarifying that the struggle was aimed at ending British colonial rule and was not directed towards the Turkish Cypriots. The problem was that its ultimate objective, the union of the island with Greece, was strongly opposed by the Turkish Cypriot community.

Preferring to remain under British rule rather than live under Greek administration, the Turkish Cypriot community rejected any association with EOKA. In fact, as the EOKA campaign grew in strength, the Turkish Cypriot community actively sided with the colonial authorities. For example, as more and more Greek Cypriots left the police force, either in solidarity with EOKA or out of fear of reprisal attacks by the movement, they were replaced by Turkish Cypriot officers. This in turn fed resentment among Greek Cypriots and led to accusations—at least partially true—that the British colonial authorities were engaged in a policy of divide and rule by deliberately fomenting division between the Greek and Turkish Cypriot communities to strengthen their own position on this island. Meanwhile, the growing strength of the EOKA campaign led the Turkish Cypriots to retaliate and form a countermovement to oppose enosis. At first, their aim was either to either keep the island under British rule or else have it ceded to Turkey. Later on, they sought to partition the island between Greece and Turkey, a policy known as *taksim*. To pursue these ambitions, they formed an organisation called Volkan (Volcano), which employed guerrilla tactics similar to those of the EOKA. Later on, the organisation was restructured with support from Turkey and changed its name to the Turkish Resistance Movement (often referred to by its Turkish acronym, TMT).

HOW DID BRITAIN RESPOND TO THE UPRISING?

By the summer of 1955, the EOKA uprising was in full swing. In August, the United Kingdom invited Greece and Turkey to attend a conference on peace and security in the eastern Mediterranean. Although not directly stated, the real purpose of the event, to discuss Cyprus, was well known. It was an important moment. Britain now appeared to admit that Cyprus was not purely an internal matter after all. Instead, it directly involved the two countries, which were widely perceived by the Greek and Turkish Cypriots to be their 'motherlands'. However, Makarios was furious about the invitation to Turkey. He accused London of reigniting a Turkish interest in Cyprus thirty years after Ankara had given up its claim to Cyprus under the Treaty of Lausanne and refused to attend. The talks went ahead anyway but were beset by violent anti-Greek riots in the Turkish cities of Istanbul and Izmir. The conference soon broke down.

Britain now decided to take a tougher approach to security. The civilian governor of the island was recalled, and in his place London installed the former chief of the imperial staff, Field Marshal Sir John Harding. True to military form, Harding soon set to work radically altering the United Kingdom's approach to the problem. In addition to increasing the number of troops in the island, he introduced tough new measures, such as the internment of suspected EOKA members and the death penalty for a range of offences. However, he also recognised the need for dialogue and established negotiations with Makarios. They went nowhere. The archbishop remained determined to pursue enosis at all costs, and Britain was unwilling to leave, primarily for its own strategic reasons but also because it did not wish to antagonise Turkey by accepting the transfer of sovereignty to Greece. After five months of discussions, during which there was no drop in the level of violence, the decision was taken, in early March 1956, to deport the archbishop to the Seychelles. The hope was that this would encourage the emergence of a more moderate leadership of the Greek Cypriot community. It didn't.

WHAT WERE THE ZÜRICH-LONDON AGREEMENTS?
At this point, the British government enlisted the aid of the eminent jurist Lord Radcliffe to draft a new plan for

self-government. Simultaneously, Harding went on an all-out offensive against EOKA. Troop numbers were increased, and by the autumn of 1956 the island was buzzing as thirty thousand British soldiers attempted to defeat Colonel Grivas and his forces. It was all to no avail. In December 1956, Radcliffe's ideas for self-government were immediately rejected by Greece and the Greek Cypriots as they did not lead to enosis. Matters were complicated by the fact that, at the same time as releasing the proposals, the British government had acknowledged that the Turkish Cypriots also had a separate right of self-determination. From this moment, the Turkish Cypriots were officially and effectively upgraded from minority status to a full community.

By now, Britain had realised that the military campaign was not working. Further talks were needed. Makarios was freed from his exile and went to live in Greece, and Harding was replaced by a civilian governor, Sir Hugh Foot, who formulated an idea for self-government, while freezing the idea of self-determination. This time, the proposal was rejected by the Turkish Cypriots and Turkey on the grounds that they felt that it would nevertheless lead to the island's eventual union with Greece. They wanted partition. A few months later, in June 1958, yet another proposal was put forward, the Macmillan Plan. This called for the United Kingdom, Greece, and Turkey to take joint responsibility for the administration of the island for seven years, after which a decision would be taken on the future of Cyprus. The plan was immediately rejected by Greece and the Greek Cypriots, who saw the plan as a first step towards partition of the island as any final agreement would require Ankara's assent, and it would never accept full *enosis*.

By late 1958 the internal situation had deteriorated significantly. Successive peace proposals had been rejected, the

EOKA campaign was now in its fourth year, and the Turkish Cypriots had in that time mustered a considerable number of men and arms under the Turkish Resistance Movement. The prospect of a civil war between the two communities looked increasingly likely, which in turn could lead to conflict between Greece and Turkey. A war between Athens and Ankara—two NATO allies—could have catastrophic consequences because it would open the way for the Soviet Union to extend its control in the eastern Mediterranean. It was against this backdrop that in September 1958, Makarios announced that independence, rather than enosis, would be an acceptable solution for Cyprus. This paved the way for a meeting between representatives of the Greek and Turkish governments in Zürich in January 1959. There they agreed to endorse the creation of an independent state with powers divided between the Greek and Turkish communities living on the island. This decision was confirmed the following month at a second conference held in London, which also included representatives from Britain and the two Cypriot communities. On 16 August 1960, a year and a half after the Zürich-London Agreements were first signed, the British flag was lowered, and the Republic of Cyprus officially came into being.

HOW DID THE 1960 CONSTITUTION DIVIDE POWERS BETWEEN THE COMMUNITIES?

The new Republic of Cyprus had a complex constitutional structure that was specifically designed to balance power between the Greek and Turkish Cypriot communities in a way that would prevent the numerically much smaller Turkish Cypriot population from being sidelined by Greek Cypriots. At the top of the system, power was divided between the president, who would be elected by the Greek Cypriot community, and the vice president, who would be elected by the Turkish Cypriot community. They would each have significant veto rights over bills and proposals. They would also preside over the Council of Ministers. This would be made up of seven Greek Cypriot ministers and three Turkish Cypriot ministers (one of whom would hold a major appointment—defence, foreign affairs, or finance). This 70:30 ratio between the Greek Cypriots and Turkish Cypriots was also the basis for power sharing in other institutions, including the civil service and the single-chamber House of Representatives, the new state's parliament. (The one exception was in the armed forces, where the ratio would be 60:40.) In the case of the judiciary, the supreme constitutional court, the highest judicial body in the state, was made up of a Greek Cypriot judge, a Turkish Cypriot judge, and a neutral (foreign) judge, who would serve as the president of the court. In addition to the central government institutions, separate communal chambers were also established with responsibility over issues under the direct control of the two communities, such as educational, cultural, and religious matters.

The separation of the two communities was rigorously enforced under the political system. For example, in the event that the president was unable to carry out his duties or was absent from the island, he would be replaced by the president of the Greek Cypriot communal chamber. Likewise, if the vice president was incapacitated, his duties would be performed by the president of the Turkish Cypriot chamber. It was also notable that the new structures ensured that the two communities would retain strong ties with their respective 'motherlands', Greece and Turkey. For example, the Greek and Turkish flags would be flown alongside the Cypriot flag on government buildings, and most of the holidays would be based on Greek and Turkish national holidays, many of which were religious in nature. Crucially, despite the important links that would exist between the new state and Greece and Turkey, enosis and *taksim* were openly ruled out as future options for the new state.

WHAT ARE THE TREATIES OF GUARANTEE, ALLIANCE, AND ESTABLISHMENT?

To preserve the political order established by the 1960 constitution, Britain, Greece, and Turkey signed the Treaty of Guarantee—thereby becoming known as the guarantor powers. Through this agreement, the three countries undertook to protect the 'sovereignty, territorial integrity and independence' of the new state and were given an explicit right of intervention if the political situation on the island was challenged internally or externally. While it was expected that this right of intervention would be exercised jointly by Britain, Greece, and Turkey, article 4 of the treaty stated that if this was not possible, any of the three countries could act to restore the status quo ante—in other words, the state of affairs established under the 1960 constitution.

This agreement was strongly opposed by the Greek Cypriots on several grounds. First, many argued, the powers given to Britain, Greece, and Turkey were such that Cyprus was not truly independent. Its sovereignty was subject to external oversight and effective supervision. Second, and perhaps more important, the Treaty of Guarantee gave Turkey an explicit right to intervene in Cypriot affairs. For their part, the Turkish Cypriots believed that it was an essential element of the constitutional settlement. In the event that any steps were taken to try to change or dissolve the constitutional order created by the 1960 constitution or if an attempt was made to unite Cyprus and Greece, the Turkish government and military would be able to intervene. The Treaty of Guarantee therefore represented their ultimate guarantee against Greek Cypriot domination or the threat of enosis.

In addition to their right of intervention under the terms of the Treaty of Guarantee, Greece and Turkey were also permitted under the terms of the Treaty of Alliance, another of the three key treaties signed at the time of Cypriot independence, to maintain small military contingents on the island. The Greek force was limited to 950 personnel, and Turkey was entitled to station 650 troops on the island. The treaty also stated that the numbers could be altered upwards or downwards if so agreed by the president and vice president. Initially, these forces would be used to train the Cypriot army. At the same time, the treaty, which was signed between Cyprus, Greece, and Turkey, also envisaged that the three would work together for common defence of Cyprus and expected joint action if the territorial integrity of the republic was challenged.

Under the terms of the Treaty of Establishment, the third of the treaties, Britain was allowed to retain 99 square miles of the island as sovereign territory for military purposes. The "sovereign bases areas", (or SBAs) as they are known, are divided into two main parts. In the east of the island, near Larnaca, there is an army garrison at Dhekeleia and a listening post at Ayios Nikolaos. In the west, near Limassol, there is an army abase at Episkopi and an air force base at Akrotiri. (The location and full extent of the bases can be seen on the map at the start of this book.) At the same time, Britain was granted continued access to a number of other military facilities around the island. Over the years, many of these latter sites have been relinquished, but the main base areas remain under British control.

2

CONSTITUTIONAL COLLAPSE, 1960–1974

WHAT DID THE TWO COMMUNITIES THINK OF THEIR NEW STATE?

The reactions of the two communities to independence were rather different. By and large, the Greek Cypriot community greeted independence with a mixture of emotions ranging from indifference to outright hostility. For the large majority of Greek Cypriots, independence was regarded as a bitter defeat. The new state commanded little if any of their loyalty. Indeed, many regarded independence as a temporary measure, to be tolerated until circumstances changed and Cyprus could formally become a part of Greece. This general desire for unification was felt not only among the people but also by the Greek Cypriot leaders, including Archbishop Makarios, the island's first president. Despite the constitutional prohibitions on enosis and *taksim*, many times he publicly stated his wish to see Cyprus unite with Greece. The generally negative attitude of the Greek Cypriot community towards the new republic was further compounded by the significant powers that had been given to the Turkish Cypriot community under the constitution. Most Greek Cypriots deeply resented the fact that not only had they been denied enosis, they had also been forced to have to share power with a community that represented less that one-fifth of the population.

In contrast, the Turkish Cypriots were largely in favour of the new republic. They recognized that they had been given a significant say in the governance of the state and that their position on the island was protected by Turkey. And while they may have also harboured a degree of resentment that their hopes for partition had not been realized, they nevertheless knew that things could have been much worse. Though they were not to be a part of Turkey, neither were they a part of Greece. To this extent, the view of the Turkish Cypriots towards the new state should be read as one of relative ambivalence. Like the Greek Cypriots, they had little intrinsic loyalty to the new state. But as far as second-best options went, it represented a relatively good outcome. And there were many within the community who believed that the new state of affairs was temporary. Given that the Greek Cypriots still wanted to pursue enosis and that Turkey might (they thought) still step in to divide the island, many Turkish Cypriots continued to believe that the Republic of Cyprus could not, or would not, last. They saw *taksim* as a real possibility.

HOW DID THE CONSTITUTION BREAK DOWN?

Given the deep divisions that had developed between the two communities during the EOKA campaign (1955–59), and the relative lack of loyalty they both felt towards the new state, it always seemed unlikely that the complex governmental structure would work efficiently and effectively. There simply was not the trust and willingness to cooperate that were necessary for the new institutions to succeed. As a result, problems emerged very soon after independence. For example, questions arose concerning the composition of the army. As mentioned above, the armed forces would be split 60:40 between Greek and Turkish Cypriots. While this numerical division was accepted by the two communities, the way in which it would be implemented was strongly contested. The Greek Cypriots wished to ensure that all military units were mixed. Believing that this would allow the Greek Cypriots to overpower and neutralise their personnel if fighting broke out, the Turkish Cypriots insisted that the army be made up of separate Greek and Turkish Cypriot units.

The most significant area of disagreement between the two communities—and the one that is most often blamed for the constitutional collapse—concerned the establishment of separate Greek and Turkish Cypriot municipalities in the main towns and cities of the island. These were supposed to be established following independence. As not all Turkish Cypriots lived in separate parts of the towns, however, they proved very difficult to implement. As a result, the Greek Cypriots leadership suggested that unified Greek and Turkish Cypriot municipalities be established initially. Following this, and when feasible, steps could be taken to create ethnically separate municipalities. The Turkish Cypriots insisted that separate municipalities first be established. Once this had happened, steps could be taken to examine and rectify any problems that arose.

WHAT WERE THE THIRTEEN CONSTITUTIONAL AMENDMENTS PROPOSED BY MAKARIOS?

After more than a year of negotiations between the two communities over municipalities, President Makarios decided that the issue could be resolved only by introducing a much broader range of constitutional amendments that would alter the relationship between the two communities and, in his opinion, enable the smoother running of the government. Of course, such ideas were extremely risky. During his first visit to Ankara, in November 1962, the Turkish government had explicitly warned him that any attempt to alter the constitution would be treated with utmost seriousness. Makarios then approached the Greek government. It, too, advised against meddling with the constitution. In a secret letter sent to Makarios in April 1963, Greek Foreign Minister Evangelos Averoff-Tositsas emphasised that an attempt to alter the 1960 agreements could lead to a breakdown in relations between the Greek and Turkish Cypriots and a much wider conflict between Greece and Turkey.

Undeterred by these words of caution, the archbishop moved forward with his plans to amend the constitution. An opportunity to act came that summer when the government of Constantine Karamanlis fell. Makarios immediately got to work on drafting a final set of points to present to the Turkish Cypriots and the three guarantor powers: Britain, Greece and Turkey. As part of this effort, he sought advice from Sir Frank Soskice, an eminent British lawyer, on the legality of intervention by one of the guarantor powers in response to such a change. Soskice argued that an intervention would not be legal if articles of the constitution were left unimplemented, such as the provision for separate municipalities. However, action would be justified if constitutional amendments were made that could have a substantive effect on the security of the Turkish Cypriots. Again, the advice appeared to underscore how risky the proposed changes were. Nevertheless, Makarios had made up his mind. On 17 November, and after having consulted the British high commissioner (ambassador) in Nicosia, who is widely believed to have helped to edit them, he sent a copy of his proposed amendments to British

Prime Minister Sir Alec Douglas-Home for his inspection prior to officially submitting the plan to the Turkish Cypriots and the guarantor powers. Receiving no rejection or warning from London, on 29 November the archbishop issued his plans for a thirteen-point amendment to the constitution. The proposals were as follows:

1. The right of veto of the president and the vice president of the republic to be abandoned.
2. The vice president of the Republic to deputise for the president of the republic in case of his temporary absence or incapacity to perform his duties.
3. The Greek president of the House of Representatives and the Turkish vice president to be elected by the House as a whole and not as at present the president by the Greek members of the House and the vice president by the Turkish members.
4. The vice president of the House of Representatives to deputise for the president of the House in case of his temporary absence or incapacity to perform his duties.
5. The constitutional provisions regarding separate majorities for enactment of certain laws by the House of Representatives to be abolished.
6. Unified municipalities to be established.
7. The administration of justice to be unified.
8. The division of the security forces into police and gendarmerie to be abolished.
9. The numerical strength of the security forces and of the defence forces to be determined by law.
10. The proportion of the participation of Greek and Turkish Cypriots in the composition of the public service and the forces of the republic to be modified in proportion to the ratio of the population of Greek and Turkish Cypriots.

11. The number of the members of the Public Service Commission to be reduced from ten to five.

12. All decisions of the Public Service Commission to be taken by simple majority.

13. The Greek Communal Chamber to be abolished.

HOW DID FIGHTING START BETWEEN THE TWO COMMUNITIES IN 1963, AND WAS IT PLANNED?

Less than two weeks after the proposed amendments were presented, Turkey rejected them. Despite assurances given by Makarios that the amendments were solely designed to promote a smoother working of the constitution, the plans severely undermined Turkish Cypriot political power in the Republic of Cyprus. After Ankara's decision, tensions rapidly arose between the two communities. On 21 December, 1963, tempers boiled over when some Turkish Cypriots were stopped at a late-night Greek Cypriot roadblock in Nicosia. Within hours, large numbers of Turkish Cypriots had taken to the streets of the capital to protest. This in turn led to violent clashes with Greek Cypriots. Very soon, armed confrontations were reported in other towns, such as Limassol and Kyrenia. Days later, the violence had spread across the whole island. In the months that followed, the fighting continued, and many people were forced from their homes, sometimes as part of a policy of ethnic cleansing. However, many Turkish Cypriots chose to congregate in enclaves, where they could be protected by Turkish and Turkish Cypriot forces.

One question that is often asked about these events is the degree to which they were organised as part of a plot to bring down the Cypriot state. On balance, it would seem that they were. The difficulty is in trying to decide which side was to blame. As has been noted, hard-liners in both communities bitterly opposed the 1960 constitutional settlement and sought to undermine it, by violence if necessary. Many have suggested that there was a coordinated and structured blueprint on the Greek Cypriot side to use violence to remove the Turkish Cypriots from the central government—a proposal known as the Akritas Plan. Similarly, it seems highly likely that on the Turkish Cypriot side many former members of the TMT were determined to destabilise the situation in the hope, or expectation, that Turkey would in fact invade and that this would lead to formal partition. However, the exact role of these groups in the events that led to the collapse of the first and only mixed government of the Republic of Cyprus has never been fully uncovered.

DID THE TURKISH CYPRIOTS WITHDRAW FROM GOVERNMENT, OR WERE THEY FORCED OUT?

One of the first consequences of the fighting was the end of Turkish Cypriot involvement in the state institutions. The question of whether they opted to leave or were coerced remains one of the most controversial in modern Cypriot history. The Turkish Cypriots are adamant that once the fighting started between the two communities they were systematically expelled from the government by the Greek Cypriots. The Greek Cypriots take a very different view. They insist that the Turkish Cypriots withdrew from the government of the Republic of Cyprus to set up their own parallel administration. As is often the case in these situations, the truth lies between the two positions. It is clear that in some areas, though by no means all, Turkish Cypriots were prevented by Greek Cypriots from travelling to work and even from entering government buildings. However, many others chose to withdraw from the government in response to calls by the Turkish Cypriot leadership to do so. At the same time, some Turkish Cypriots who wished to continue to work as part of the government were prevented from doing so by Turkish Cypriot militias. A few Turkish Cypriots did manage to continue working and participating in the government. It is also worth noting that in some areas, such as Famagusta, where the local leaders of both sides were more moderate than elsewhere and where fighting was much lighter, Turkish Cypriots continued to work with Greek Cypriots for a while after the fighting started.

HOW DID THE UN ESTABLISH A PEACEKEEPING PRESENCE ON THE ISLAND?

Almost as soon as the clashes started, Turkey began preparing for a military invasion. Fearing that this could lead to a major confrontation between Athens and Ankara, the British government managed to persuade the other two guarantor powers to form a small peacekeeping mission—the Joint Truce Force—in the hope that this would hold the line while Britain put together a peace conference in London. While the force did manage to dampen the fighting in many places, its success was hampered by the fact that neither the Greek nor the Turkish military contingents based on the island participated as fully as they were meant to. This meant that almost the entire burden of responsibility for quelling the clashes fell on the British army. And while reinforcements were sent from Britain, in January and February 1964, numerous other conflicts around the world meant the United Kingdom could not manage the sort of commitment required to keep the force going indefinitely. To make matters worse, as the weeks passed, Greek Cypriots became increasingly suspicious of Britain's intentions. The EOKA campaign had ended only a few years earlier, and many Greek Cypriots believed that the British soldiers were sympathetic to the Turkish Cypriots. Following the failure of the London peace conference held in January 1964, Britain's position as a peacekeeper became untenable, and it began to look around for a possible replacement. Although the Greek Cypriots favoured some form of UN involvement, this option was rejected on the grounds that it would give the Soviet Union a direct say over the island. The British and U.S. governments preferred a peacekeeping force formed from NATO member states. Makarios rejected this idea; he felt that in view of Turkey's strategic importance to the Western alliance, such a force would be more sympathetic to the Turkish Cypriots. Makarios solicited help from the Soviet Union, which wrote to the leaders of Britain, Greece, Turkey, and the United States, stating that sending a NATO force to the island would be unacceptable given that Cyprus was not a member of the alliance and had actually adopted a strategy of nonalignment. As a result of this diplomatic intervention, which threatened to create a crisis in the eastern Mediterranean, Britain was eventually forced to relent and take the matter to the United Nations. Several weeks later, on 4 March 1964, the UN Security Council passed Resolution 186. This established the United Nation Force in Cyprus (UNFICYP).

WHY IS UN SECURITY COUNCIL RESOLUTION 186 SO IMPORTANT?

In addition to establishing the peacekeeping force, Resolution 186 was important in two other ways. First, its references to the government of Cyprus confirmed that despite the absence of

the Turkish Cypriots, an internationally recognised administration still existed. In other words, it recognised the Greek
Cypriots as having effective control over the functions and
institutions of the Republic of Cyprus. This situation persists
to this day and is deeply resented by the Turkish Cypriots,
who argue that there can be no government of Cyprus without
them and that the internationally recognised administration
is actually illegal.

Second, the UN was also assigned responsibility for
managing the peacemaking process. Specifically, the UN
Security Council recommended that U Thant, then secretary-
general, in consultation with the parties and the guarantor
powers, designate a mediator to take charge of formal negotiation efforts. Shortly afterwards, he appointed Sakari
Tuomioja, a Finnish diplomat, to the post. Although Tuomioja
viewed the problem on the island as international in nature,
involving Greece and Turkey, and saw enosis as the most
logical option for the island, he did not pursue the idea as he
believed that it would have been inappropriate for a UN official to propose a solution that would lead to the dissolution of
a UN member state. His work was tragically cut short just
months later when he died suddenly.

Galo Plaza Lasso, a former president of Ecuador, was
appointed as his replacement. Taking a tough approach, in
March 1965 he unveiled a sixty-six-page report that criticised
both sides for not having shown enough commitment to
reaching a settlement. It also made some strong and unpalat-
able recommendations. Plaza Lasso believed that enosis
should be abandoned for the meanwhile. At the same time, he
asserted that Turkish Cypriots should abandon their demands
for a federal solution and accept Greek Cypriot majority rule.
Although the Greek Cypriots eventually accepted the report,

despite its opposition to immediate enosis, Turkey and the Turkish Cypriots reacted angrily. Arguing that his role was to broker an agreement, not submit proposals, they called for him to resign. In response, the Greek Cypriots insisted that if he did step down they would refuse to accept a replacement. Given this deadlock, U Thant had to abandon the mediation effort. When Plaza Lasso did eventually resign at the end of 1965, he was not replaced. Formally speaking, there has never been another 'UN mediator.' There have, however, been many further UN mediation attempts.

WHAT WAS THE ACHESON PLAN?

While the UN was assigned primary responsibility for peace-making, the United States also decided to try its hand at brokering an agreement. In early June 1964, Turkish intervention was averted only by a harshly worded warning from President Johnson. Washington launched an independent initiative under Dean Acheson, who had been secretary of state during the Truman administration. In July Acheson presented a plan to unite Cyprus with Greece. In return, Turkey would receive a sovereign military base on the island, rather in the same way that Britain had been given a base in 1960, and the Turkish Cypriots would be given strong minority rights that would be overseen and protected by a resident international commissioner. Makarios quickly rejected the U.S. proposal on the grounds that a sovereign Turkish base on the island would limit enosis and would give Ankara too strong a say in the island's affairs. Soon afterwards a second version of the plan was presented that offered Turkey a fifty-year lease on a base rather than full sovereignty. This time the offer was rejected by both the Greek Cypriots and by Turkey. After several further unsuccessful attempts to refine the plan, Washington gave up its effort.

HOW DID THE UN MISSION OF GOOD OFFICES EMERGE?

Despite the failure of the formal mediation effort, U Thant nevertheless decided to continue the search for a solution to the island's political problems. This time, though, he adopted a much less overt and less high-handed approach. In 1966 he made his Good Offices available to the two sides under the auspices of Carlos Bernades, a Brazilian diplomat who was serving as the UN secretary-general's special representative for Cyprus. Instead of trying to develop formal proposals for the parties to bargain over, Bernades aimed to encourage the two sides to agree to settlement through direct dialogue. His initial efforts were thwarted by political chaos in Greece that eventually resulted in the April 1967 military coup d'état. At first, there was optimism that this might actually open the way for a solution in Cyprus because the new military administration appeared determined to settle the issue. In early September 1967, the Greek and Turkish foreign ministers met for two meetings on either side of their border in Thrace. The talks were a fiasco. Although Washington had suggested that the Turkish government might be willing to consider enosis, when the idea was actually suggested Ankara immediately and categorically rejected it. Greece was now forced to abandon the idea of union for the foreseeable future.

Two months later, in November 1967, Cyprus experienced another serious bout of intercommunal fighting. Responding to a major attack by Greek Cypriots on Turkish Cypriot villages in the south of the island, which left twenty-seven people dead, Turkey bombed Greek Cypriot forces and once again appeared to be readying for an invasion. In response, Greece agreed to recall General George Grivas, the cofounder of EOKA, who had been serving as the commander of the Greek Cypriot National Guard, and to reduce its forces on the island. The Turkish Cypriots used the opportunity to announce that they had formed their own provisional administration. Although Makarios denounced the move as illegal, it was nevertheless clear that the political situation on the ground had changed.

The Archbishop, along with most other Greek Cypriots, now began to accept that the Turkish Cypriots would have to have some degree of political autonomy. Makarios also realised that enosis was not possible under the prevailing circumstances and that Cyprus would remain an independent state. In May 1968, talks once again resumed, this time under the auspices of the Good Offices of the UN Secretary-General. While the Turkish Cypriots were prepared to make concessions regarding constitutional changes, Makarios had difficulty accepting the idea that they should have greater autonomy. Nevertheless, the negotiations continued over the next six years and at one point, an agreement appeared to be on the horizon. But such hopes were dashed by the turbulent events of 1974.

WHAT LED TO THE GREEK MILITARY COUP IN CYPRUS?

While armed clashes between Greek and Turkish Cypriots subsided after 1967, a dangerous new conflict had arisen within the Greek Cypriot community. Although Makarios had decided to abandon enosis in favour of a more realistic approach, many Greek Cypriots remained deeply wedded to the idea. In September 1971, Grivas secretly returned to the island and formed EOKA-B, a vehemently pro-union organisation. Over the next few years it waged a terrorist campaign against the Makarios administration, even launching several assassination attempts against the archbishop himself. In early 1974 matters came to a head when Grivas died and EOKA-B came under the direct control of Brigadier Dimitrios Ioannidis, the brutal new leader of the Greek military junta. Fearing that the Greek army would now try to overthrow him, Makarios wrote an open letter to the military dictatorship requesting that all Greek officers be removed from Cyprus. Ioannidis refused and ordered Greek forces on the island to oust the archbishop.

On 15 July 1974, Greek and Greek Cypriot forces began firing on the presidential palace in Nicosia. Even though he appeared to be surrounded, Makarios escaped the city and made his way to Paphos, in the southwest of the island. From there he was taken by British troops to RAF Akrotiri and flown to London, where he had meetings with British officials before travelling on to the United Nations headquarters in New York. Meanwhile, back on the island, Nicos Sampson, a former EOKA gunman who had taken part in attacks against Turkish Cypriots in 1964 and was a known supporter of union between Greece and Cyprus, took over as the head of the Cypriot administration.

HOW DID THE TURKISH INVASION HAPPEN?
Sampson's appointment as the head of the Greek military-backed administration in Cyprus left many observers with little doubt that a declaration of enosis was imminent. The Turkish government started planning its response. Bulent Ecevit, the Turkish prime minister, flew to London to see if Britain would

be willing to intervene jointly under the terms of the Treaty of Guarantee. The British government declined, arguing that it was ill prepared for such a major action. Ecevit therefore decided that the Turkish armed forces would have to act on their own. He ordered a full-scale invasion of the island. Just after 6 o'clock in the morning, on 20 July 1974, Turkish fighter planes began bombing strategic locations near Nicosia, and paratroops were dropped along the Kyrenia mountain range. An hour later, the first boatloads of Turkish soldiers landed on the northern shores of the island. Working in conjunction with the Turkish Cypriot militias, they attempted to establish a corridor linking the coast with the Turkish Cypriot suburbs of Nicosia, in the centre of the island. Putting up stiff resistance, the Greek Cypriot National Guard managed to slow their advance. However, they could not stop it. Within two days, the Turkish Army had managed to establish a meagre, but nevertheless secure, foothold on the island.

Internationally, the invasion prompted a strong response. Both the United States and Britain issued statements condemning Turkey's actions but harshly criticising the Greek military administration for precipitating the crisis. At the United Nations, the Security Council passed a resolution calling for the immediate end of foreign military intervention and the withdrawal of all forces other than those covered by the relevant treaties. Meanwhile, the successful Turkish invasion led to turmoil in Athens. On 23 July, the military junta collapsed and was replaced by a civilian government under Constantine Karamanlis, a veteran Greek statesman. Likewise, Sampson was forced to step down. This in turn paved the way for the start of formal peace talks in Geneva between the three guarantor powers. At the talks the Turkish government agreed to halt its advance on the condition that it would remain on the island until a political settlement was reached between the two sides. Soon afterwards, on 8 August, a second round of talks was convened, this time including representatives of the island's two main communities. During the discussions the Turkish Cypriots, supported by Turkey, insisted on an immediate response to their demand for a federal settlement. When the Greek Cypriot delegation asked for a delay to consult with Makarios in New York, Ankara seized the opportunity to resume its offensive.

On 14 August the second wave of the invasion began. Fanning out east and west from the narrow wedge of territory they had captured in the first round of fighting, Turkish forces rapidly overran most of the north of the island as tens of thousands of Greek Cypriots fled their homes. The United Nations Security Council passed several more resolutions deploring the fighting and calling on all parties to respect the sovereignty, territorial integrity, and independence of the Republic of Cyprus, but Ankara continued with its operation. In the end, it took three days to put in place a new—this time, permanent—cease-fire. By then Turkey had captured 36 percent of the island.

WAS THE TURKISH INVASION LEGAL?

The events surrounding the Greek military coup and the Turkish invasion in 1974 are hotly contested by the two communities. One of the most controversial questions concerns the legality of Turkey's decision to intervene. For the Greek Cypriots it was a premeditated and illegal act of aggression. The Turkish Cypriots regard it as a legitimate and necessary step to prevent enosis and protect them against the Greek Cypriots. In coming to any conclusions about the invasion, it is necessary to consider the two waves separately. The operation staged in response to the Greek military coup can be seen to be broadly legal under the terms of the Treaty of Guarantee. As required, Turkey consulted with Britain following the coup. Ankara was therefore within its powers when it decided to stage a unilateral operation. Where the problem arises is with regard to the second and subsequent invasion in August 1974. Staged after the failure of the coup in Cyprus, it is clear that this operation was not intended to return to the situation created in 1960. Instead, it was obviously designed to pave the way for a radically different settlement. The balance of history, and the view of most informed observers, is that while the first invasion was legitimate, the second invasion was wholly contrary to international law.

A common related question is whether the Turkish invasion was part of a wider conspiracy that involved the government of the United States and, to a lesser extent, the British government. Many Greek Cypriots strongly believe that it was. As they see it, the Turkish government would never have been willing to intervene without clear authorisation from Washington. However, they have no evidence to support this view. Recent research conducted by independent scholars with access to the extensive British and American archives has painted a very different story. (The sheer enormity of the archives makes it very difficult to believe that the papers could all have been uniformly doctored to present a false picture of events.) Rather than a conspiracy, they detail a complex picture of misunderstandings, misinterpretations, and political upheaval. It is worth bearing in mind that the Cyprus invasion took place at the height of the Watergate scandal—which eventually led to the resignation of President Richard Nixon. During this period, U.S. foreign policy was being overseen by Henry Kissinger, the secretary of state and national security advisor. Although many Greek Cypriots like to view Kissinger as an 'evil genius' masterminding the invasion, the evidence suggests that he was rather ill informed about events on the island. His primary concern was to prevent a war between Greece and Turkey. Moreover, the archives show that in the early months of 1974 the Nixon administration on the whole believed that Greece would not overthrow Makarios and that Turkey would not invade even if Greece did oust him.

As for the accusation that Britain was involved in the plot, again there is strong counterevidence. Records show that the British government in fact tried to persuade Washington to mount a defence of the island against the Turkish invasion. This idea was rebuffed by the Nixon administration, which did not want to make war against a strategically vital ally. Without U.S. support, Britain was willing only to mount a strong defence of the Nicosia airport, the headquarters of the UN Force in Cyprus. This prevented the Turkish military from securing a valuable airfield for its invasion and brought the United Kingdom very close to an armed conflict with Turkey. Nevertheless, and despite the weight of evidence to the contrary, the idea persists that the 1974 invasion was part of a larger British-American conspiracy.

3

A DIVIDED ISLAND, 1974–

WHAT WERE THE EFFECTS OF THE INVASION ON THE TWO COMMUNITIES?

The invasion and division of the island had a profound effect on both communities. But for the Greek Cypriots the effects were particularly catastrophic. The Turkish military operation left thousands dead or wounded and many more missing. (In recent years the UN Committee for Missing Persons has worked to identify the remains of many who went missing, but more than a thousand have yet to be accounted for.) In addition, many Greek Cypriots—those living along the entire north coast; along the Karpas peninsula; and in Varosha, the predominantly Greek Cypriot region of the eastern port city of Famagusta—were forced to leave their homes. In total, approximately 160,000 people were displaced.

At the same time, the invasion had disastrous consequences for the economy. Statistics provided by the Government of Cyprus show that the invasion led to a 70 percent drop in the gross output of the country and a 30 percent rise in unemployment. Important farming areas—such as Morphou, the home of the island's citrus industry—were now under Turkish and Turkish Cypriot control as was most of the island's tourism accommodation. Just under half of industrial production, and over half of all mining output, was also gone. The important port of Famagusta was lost, as was the main international airport in Nicosia, which was now in the UN-controlled buffer zone. In human terms the effects were profound. A report produced by the University of Cyprus in July 2010 estimates that the total value of Greek Cypriot private land (not government land or church property) in the north is US $82.1 billion at 2009 prices. The loss of earnings from the lack of access to this land has been put at US $15.78 billion.

For the Turkish Cypriots, the effects of the Turkish intervention were more positive. Throughout the 1960s they had been in a rather precarious position. Since the outbreak of intercommunal fighting, large numbers had been living in enclaves under an effective state of siege. Greek Cypriot forces had at times even prevented food and medicine from getting through. Now, however, they were in control of a large portion of the island. In the months after the invasion around fifty thousand Turkish Cypriots who had been living in the south relocated to the areas under Turkish and Turkish Cypriot control in the north. To house them, the Turkish Cypriot authorities expropriated the abandoned Greek Cypriot properties and redistributed them to Turkish Cypriots. (For the sake of comparison, the same University of Cyprus report estimated that during the period 1974–1997 Turkish Cypriots' losses from the lack of use of their land in the south were US $2.2 billion.) Meanwhile, starting shortly after the invasion, settlers from mainland Turkey began arriving on the island. They, too, were given Greek Cypriot properties.

WHAT WERE THE 'HIGH-LEVEL AGREEMENTS'?

In addition to its human effects, the invasion of course also had important political ramifications. For a start, enosis was finally dead. With more than a third of the island in their hands, the Turkish Cypriots now had absolutely no reason to accept the island's union with Greece. Moreover, any hope that Cyprus could continue as a unitary state was quashed. The Turkish Cypriots need now accept nothing less than a federation. Indeed, in February 1975 they announced the formation of the Turkish Federated State of Northern Cyprus. Two months later, in April 1975, the UN tried to restart talks, though it met with little success. At the beginning of 1977, it tried again. This time there was a breakthrough. On 12 February, the leaders of the two communities, Makarios and Rauf Denktash, reached a four-point agreement (the first high-level agreement) defining the terms of reunification:

1. We are seeking an independent, non-aligned, bi-communal Federal Republic.
2. The territory under the administration of each community should be discussed in the light of economic viability or productivity and land ownership.
3. Questions of principles like freedom of movement, freedom of settlement, the right of property and other specific matters, are open for discussion, taking into consideration the fundamental basis of a bi-communal federal system and certain practical difficulties which may arise for the Turkish Cypriot Community.
4. The powers and functions of the central federal government will be such as to safeguard the unity of the country having regard to the bi-communal character of the State.

Using this agreement as a starting point, the United States, Britain, and Canada drafted a twelve-point proposal for a federation of two states, one of which would be predominantly Greek Cypriot and the other mainly Turkish Cypriot. Although the terms of the draft, which was presented to the two sides by the UN, appeared to be broadly in line with the 1977 agreement, the Greek Cypriots rejected it. In particular, they were unhappy that the plan did not enshrine the three basic freedoms that they insisted must be part of any 'just and viable' settlement: the freedom of movement, the freedom of settlement, and the right to own property. The UN remained undeterred. In May 1979, Kurt Waldheim, the UN secretary-general, visited Cyprus and brokered a second high-level agreement between Denktash and Spyros Kyprianou, who had succeeded Makarios as president of Cyprus following the archbishop's death in August 1977. This subsequent agreement was made up of ten points:

1. It was agreed to resume the intercommunal talks on 15 June 1979.
2. The basis for the talks will be the Makarios-Denktash guidelines of 12 February 1977 and the UN resolutions relevant to the Cyprus question.
3. There should be respect for human rights and fundamental freedoms of all citizens of the Republic.
4. The talks will deal with all territorial and constitutional aspects.
5. Priority will be given to reaching agreement of the resettlement of Varosha under UN auspices simultaneously with the beginning of the consideration by the interlocutors of the constitutional and territorial aspects of a comprehensive settlement. After agreement on Varosha

has been reached it will be implemented without awaiting the outcome of the discussion on other aspects of the Cyprus problem.

6. It was agreed to abstain from any action which might jeopardize the outcome of the talks, and special importance will be given to initial practical measures by both sides to promote goodwill, mutual confidence and the return to normal conditions.

7. The demilitarization of the Republic of Cyprus is envisaged, and matters relating thereto will be discussed.

8. The independence, sovereignty, territorial integrity and non-alignment of the Republic should be adequately guaranteed against union in whole or in part with any other country and against any form of partition or secession.

9. The intercommunal talks will be carried out in a continuing and sustained matter, avoiding any delay.

10. The intercommunal talks will take place in Nicosia.

WHEN AND WHY DID THE TURKISH CYPRIOTS UNILATERALLY DECLARE INDEPENDENCE?

In the years immediately following the high-level agreements, the United Nations continued its efforts to broker a settlement, but without success. While the two sides may have agreed in principle to reunification under a federal system, they remained far apart in terms of the practical elements of such a system. This deadlock was only magnified when, on 15 November 1983, the Turkish Cypriot administration, in a surprise move, unilaterally declared independence. While the Turkish government quickly announced that it recognised the Turkish Republic of Northern Cyprus (TRNC), as the new entity was called, the Turkish Cypriot decision was roundly condemned by the international community. Meeting just days later, the UN Security Council passed Resolution 541, which stated that the declaration was legally invalid and should be withdrawn. It also instructed UN members to continue to recognise the sovereignty, independence, and territorial integrity of the Republic of Cyprus as the only internationally recognised state on the island. The TRNC has subsequently not been recognised by any state apart from Turkey.

Quite why the Turkish Cypriots chose to declare independence has never been fully answered. In large part, it appears to have reflected the personal ambition of Rauf Denktash, the hard-line separatist Turkish Cypriot leader, to be the founder of a Turkish Cypriot state. As it was always unlikely that the move would be recognised by the international community, it seems as if the decision was shaped more by personal vanity than by a desire to do what was best for the Turkish Cypriot people. Indeed, many Turkish Cypriots strongly opposed the move, realising that it would ultimately harm reunification efforts and undermine any international support that they might have had. As for timing, this is an easier question to answer. The decision was directly linked to political events in Turkey, which was currently in the process of making a transition from military to civilian rule. It seemed unlikely that the new Turkish government under Turgut Ozal, who was known as a pro-Western moderniser, would have agreed to allow the declaration of independence because of the possibility that it would leave Turkey diplomatically isolated on the world stage.

WHAT WAS THE 'DRAFT FRAMEWORK AGREEMENT'?

Although the unilateral declaration of independence marked an attempt to change the facts on the ground, the Turkish

Cypriot leader insisted that it would not end efforts to find a political settlement. A little less than a year after the Turkish Cypriots declared independence, reunification talks started again. This time, it appeared as though real progress had been made. After three rounds of discussions in the winter of 1984, a blueprint was reached. Cyprus would become a bizonal, bicommunal, nonaligned federation. The Turkish Cypriot entity would amount to 29 percent of the island, and all foreign troops would leave the island. But in a final January 1985 meeting between the two leaders, Kyprianou insisted on further negotiations, and the talks soon collapsed. The Greek Cypriot leader came in for heavy criticism, both at home and abroad. For his part, Denktash walked away with a public relations victory and a reprieve. He also insisted that he would not be willing to make so many concessions in future. (However, this should not be read to mean that Denktash actually supported the plan. Apparently, he had received word that Kyprianou would reject the agreement and so was able to accept knowing that he would come out looking good.)

Despite the setback, the UN still persisted in its efforts to find a solution. In March 1986, Javier Perez de Cuellar, who had succeeded Waldheim as UN secretary-general, presented the two sides with a draft framework agreement. This plan, too, envisaged the creation of an independent, nonaligned, bicommunal, bizonal state in Cyprus. However, the Greek Cypriots were unhappy with the proposals. First, the proposal appeared to be based on a confederation rather than on a federation (this will be explored in more detail later in the book). Second, it did not address the removal of Turkish forces from the island or the repatriation of the increasing number of Turkish settlers arriving in the north. Third, the draft lacked guarantees that the three freedoms—movement, settlement, and property ownership—would be respected. Finally, Kyprianou wanted an international conference to discuss guarantees. Turkey and the Turkish Cypriots refused this last point on the grounds that neither was prepared to engage in direct discussions with the Cypriot government, an administration they considered to be illegal. Further efforts to produce an agreement failed. But, in the end, they did agree on one thing. At a series of meetings in Geneva, in 1988, the two leaders decided to abandon the draft framework agreement and return to the 1977 and 1979 high-level agreements.

WHAT WAS THE 'SET OF IDEAS'?

In August 1988, yet another round of negotiations got under way. Ten months later, in July 1989, the UN secretary-general unveiled a 'set of ideas'. Like the other proposals, this one advocated the establishment of a federation based on political equality and indivisible sovereignty, thereby outlawing partition or secession. Denktash quickly rejected it. He insisted that the Greek Cypriots recognise the existence of two peoples in Cyprus and their basic right to self-determination—a position many viewed as an attempt to open the way for a legal declaration of independence by the Turkish Cypriots after a settlement had been reached. Matters were further complicated by the Cypriot government's decision to apply to join the European Union (more on this shortly). Furious at this move, Denktash called off all talks. In his last report to the Security Council, de Cuellar laid the blame for the failure of the talks squarely on Denktash, arguing that the Turkish Cypriot leader's demand that the two communities should have equal sovereignty and a right to secession prevented further discussions.

In January 1992 Boutros Boutros-Ghali took over as UN secretary-general and decided to continue work on the 'set of ideas'. Yet again Denktash refused to talk about the proposals and repeated his criticism that the secretary-general had exceeded his authority. Although the Turkish Cypriot side had accepted 91 of 100 of the proposals, Denktash's unwillingness to engage in substantive talks on the remaining nine areas of difference meant that further progress was impossible. The incoming Greek Cypriot government, formed under Glafcos Clerides in 1993, also sought to move away from the 'set of ideas'. It was also at this point that two developments emerged that would alter the very landscape of the Cyprus problem: the Loizidou case and EU's decision to accept Cyprus as a candidate for membership.

WHAT WAS THE LOIZIDOU CASE?

A wit once said that the Cyprus issue is essentially a problem of thirty thousand Turkish troops faced off against thirty thousand Greek Cypriot lawyers. (Or, as someone else put it, while the Turkish army uses warfare, the Greek Cypriots use 'lawfare'.) Nothing highlights this standoff more clearly than the Loizidou case. In 1989, Titina Loizidou, a Greek Cypriot refugee from the northern coastal town of Kyrenia, was arrested and held for several hours by Turkish forces while participating in a rally that had attempted to cross the Green Line. Afterward, she filed a case against Turkey at the European Court of Human Rights arguing that the Turkish military occupation of the northern part of the island had deprived her of control over her property; a contravention of Article 8 of the European Convention on Human Rights, which protected the individual's right 'to respect for his private and family life, his home and his correspondence.' The Turkish government denied the claim on two counts. First, it could not be held responsible for the acts of the TRNC, which it argued was an independent state. Second, the TRNC had enacted laws that meant that the property no longer belonged to Mrs. Loizidou. The court disagreed on both counts. In a landmark ruling issue on 19 December 1996, it decided that the Turkish Cypriot authorities were in fact a 'subordinate administration'. Ankara, through the presence of large numbers of troops, was ultimately responsible for the actions of the Turkish Cypriots. It further ruled that Mrs Loizidou remained the legal owner of the land. Two years later, the court ordered Turkey to pay several hundred thousand dollars in compensation.

It was a watershed moment. By judging that Mrs Loizidou remained the lawful owner of her property and that Turkey could be held financially liable for such claims, the European Court of Human Rights (ECHR) had opened the way for lawsuits from every other Greek Cypriot refugee. The political and financial costs of such litigation would be enormous. Ankara therefore decided to reject the ruling, even though the European Union required compliance with ECHR rulings as a basic requirement for membership.

HOW DID CYPRUS BECOME A CANDIDATE FOR EU MEMBERSHIP?
Although the Loizidou ruling was a serious setback for Turkey, a far more significant development was the decision of the Greek Cypriots to apply for membership to the European Union. The island's relationship with the EU began in the early 1960s, when Cyprus first applied for an association agreement. Although this initial application was retracted, a two-stage

agreement was eventually signed in December 1972. According to the terms of the deal, in the first phase tariffs on a range of goods would be reduced. This would then lead to the second stage, a full customs union between Cyprus and the EU by 1982. Although the Turkish invasion of the island threw these plans into disarray, an additional protocol, signed in May 1987, subsequently paved the way for a full customs union by 2002. However, this was no longer enough for the Greek Cypriots. On 4 July 1990, and acting with the support of both Britain and Greece, which had become a member in 1981, the Cypriot government under President George Vassiliou formally applied for membership in the union.

The announcement came at the right time. With the Cold War at an end, the European Union was already starting to consider the possibility of a major expansion, and Cyprus was certainly seen to be a part of Europe. This was clearly reflected when the European Commission, the executive body of the European Union, issued its formal opinion (*avis*) on the application, on 30 June 1993. In it, it stated:

> Cyprus's geographical position, the deep-lying bonds which, for two thousand years, have located the island at the very fount of European culture and civilization, the intensity of the European influence apparent in the values shared by the people of Cyprus and in the conduct of the cultural, political, economic and social life of its citizens, the wealth of its contacts of every kind with the Community, all these confer on Cyprus, beyond all doubt, its European identity and character and confirm its vocation to belong to the Community.

In terms of the economic requirements for membership, and the need to conform to the *acquis communautiare*, the EU's body of laws, the commission envisaged no 'insurmountable problems'. As the report noted, 'The economy of the southern part of the island has demonstrated an ability to adapt and seems ready to face the challenge of integration provided that the work already started on reforms and on opening up to the outside world is maintained, notably in the context of the customs union.' As one might expect, the opinion also addressed the all-important question of the division of the island. On this issue, it noted that the process of accession would both shape and be shaped by efforts to reach a comprehensive solution. As the opinion explained, 'The leaders of the Turkish Cypriot community are fully conscious of the economic and social benefits that integration with Europe would bring their Community.' In other words, the accession process would assist efforts to reach a comprehensive settlement. The report nevertheless appeared to leave the door open for the possibility that a settlement might not be reached. On 25 June 1994, the member states officially confirmed that Cyprus would take part in the next wave of enlargement discussions.

WHAT WAS THE TURKISH RESPONSE TO THE EU DECISION TO ACCEPT CYPRUS AS A CANDIDATE?

The Turkish Cypriots and Turkey were furious at the decision. From the outset, they had both been strongly opposed to any move to accept Cyprus as a candidate for EU membership. In the main, their response was driven by fear. Both realised that were Cyprus to join the European Union it would almost certainly have an extremely negative effect on Turkey's own hopes of joining. The Turkish government had submitted an application for full membership three years before Cyprus, in 1987. The EU was initially unwilling to grant it formal candidacy—a decision based on a range of factors, including concerns about its political and human rights records and opposition by some member states to admitting such a large Muslim state. It now seemed possible that Cyprus would join before Turkey, and there was a real danger that it would then block Turkey's membership to try to force a solution.

Given these concerns, Ankara and the Turkish Cypriots mounted a strong campaign to prevent Cyprus from joining the European Union. In addition to taking a more hard-line position in the reunification talks in an effort to signal that they would not give in to the threat of EU accession, the Turkish government and Turkish Cypriot leaders insisted that the pace of integration between Turkey and the TRNC increase to match that of the south with the European Union. Tensions on the island also began to rise to dangerous levels. In the summer of 1996, the two sides came close to renewed conflict when a number of Greek Cypriot protestors tried to cross the Green Line dividing the two parts of the island. This was followed by an ill-judged move by the Greek Cypriots to pressure the Turkey and the Turkish Cypriots to engage in peace talks by purchasing Russian S-300 ground-to-air missile defence system. Rather than pushing talks along, this move instead meant that the international community spent eighteen months defusing a potentially disastrous crisis.

The Turkish Cypriots also adopted legal arguments to try to prevent the island's accession. They insisted that membership would violate the 1960 constitution of the Republic of Cyprus, which specifically prevents the Cypriot state from joining any organisation that has either Greece or Turkey, but not both, as members. The European Union, as they saw it, quite clearly fell into this category (Greece had been a member since 1981). However, after exhaustive legal analysis, this argument was rejected by the European Union, as well as by Britain, the third guarantor power. Instead, the European Union argued that Turkey and the Turkish Cypriots should seize the opportunity to bring about reunification of the island. Indeed, under pressure from the European Union, the Cypriot government offered the Turkish Cypriots the opportunity to send a delegation to participate in the talks. Much to the disappointment of the European Union, Denktash declined the invitation point-blank.

HOW DID THE EU ACCESSION AFFECT THE REUNIFICATION TALKS?

Formal accession negotiation started between the European Union and Cyprus in 1998. Nevertheless, the Turkish government continued to believe that there was no chance that the European Union would risk provoking a crisis with Turkey, a major state of 60 million people, in favour of eight hundred thousand Greek Cypriots. Denktash, meanwhile, was still adamant that any solution in Cyprus be based on the sovereign equality of the two communities. By late 2001, however, it was clear that the European Union was not going to back down in the face of threats. In a last ploy to try to delay EU accession, Denktash called for new talks with his Greek Cypriot counterpart, Glafcos Clerides. The Turkish Cypriot leader, fully supported by a nationalist government in Turkey, appeared to believe that if the talks appeared to go well, the EU would reconsider its position.

In November 2002 everything changed. In Turkey, the AKP (Justice and Development Party) won a landslide victory under the leadership of Recep Tayyip Erdogan. Announcing that his primary policy goal was to see Turkey join the EU, Erdogan emphasised his wish to solve the Cyprus issue. It was a monumental breakthrough, and one the UN quickly seized on by presenting the two sides with a blueprint for a settlement: the Annan Plan, named after Kofi Annan, the secretary-general. The hope was that a deal could be reached before the all-important 1 May 2004, meeting of EU leaders in Copenhagen, at which Cyprus would likely be formally invited to join the EU, along with Malta and eight states from central Europe. As had happened so many times in the past, no progress was made. Recuperating from major heart surgery, Denktash declined to meet with his Greek Cypriot counterpart or engage in meaningful talks.

Even growing pressure from within his community, which included massive street demonstrations, had little effect. Denktash remained as intransigent as ever. In a last-ditch effort to reach a settlement, Annan met with the two Cypriot leaders in The Hague and called upon them to put the latest version of the plan directly to the people in simultaneous referenda. While the idea was grudgingly accepted by Tassos Papadopoulos, a hard-line nationalist who had recently replaced the moderate Clerides as president, Denktash said no. The UN then brought its peacemaking efforts to a close. A couple of weeks later, on 16 April 2003, the Cypriot government, along with Malta and eight central and eastern European states, formally signed the treaty guaranteeing them EU membership in May 2004.

WHY WAS THE GREEN LINE OPENED?

In the weeks that followed, the Turkish Cypriot leader was heavily criticised for killing off yet another peace process. Turkey also received a clear warning that as a result of the

Turkish Cypriot leader's behaviour, its own efforts to join the EU would be obstructed. In an attempt to deflect some of this criticism, the Turkish Cypriot authorities made the completely unexpected announcement that they had decided to end the thirty-year restrictions on travel across the Green Line dividing the north and south of the island. Greek Cypriots would now be able to cross over at will as long as they showed their passport and filled in a visa slip.

Instead of welcoming the news, the Papadopoulos administration announced that it would be 'unthinkable' for Greek Cypriots to give validity to the Turkish Cypriot authorities by doing so. The administration was wrong. On the first day the border opened, 23 April 2003, an estimated five thousand people crossed the line. As word spread that the Green Line had really opened, the number of people crossing skyrocketed. In some places the Turkish Cypriot authorities could not handle the volume of people waiting to cross the line. The numbers were staggering: by early afternoon on Easter Monday, 28 April, more than fourteen thousand Greek Cypriots had crossed over at the three checkpoints that had been opened. Indeed, at one crossing the queue of vehicles stretched back 8 miles as anxious Greek Cypriot refugees waited in line to return to the North and see the homes they lost thirty years earlier. Within two weeks, two hundred thousand people—a quarter of the island's population—had crossed over, according to estimates. Perhaps most important, the atmosphere remained very good throughout. Despite the vast number of people crossing over and the dire predictions of intercommunal violence, there were almost no serious incidents. Indeed, it appeared as though all were doing their best to try to foster as positive an atmosphere as possible.

HOW DID THE FINAL VERSION OF THE ANNAN PLAN EMERGE?
While the move to open the Green Line was widely welcomed internationally and showed that the Greek and Turkish Cypriots could mix peacefully, Denktash continued to resist any calls for new negotiations. However, his position was now weakening. Turkey seemed keen to remove Cyprus as an obstacle to its EU accession process. To prove its sincerity, on 7 December 2003, the Turkish government paid more than $1 million to settle the Loizidou case. It also agreed to establish an immovable property commission to handle further Greek Cypriot claims. This was followed a week later by Turkish Cypriot parliamentary elections, which were won by the main pro-solution opposition party, the CTP (Republican Turkish Party), led by Mehmet Ali Talat. The implications of the result were obvious. While Rauf Denktash would remain the lead Turkish Cypriot negotiator by virtue of his position as leader of the Turkish Cypriot community, his moral and political position had been severely undermined. Just how much ground he had lost became clear soon afterwards when, against Denktash's wishes, Turkish prime minister Recep Tayyip Erdogan approached Annan about the possibility of new talks. Soon afterwards, the UN secretary-general summoned Papadopoulos and Denktash to New York. Just days later, on 13 February 2004, and under considerable international pressure, the two leaders reluctantly agreed to resume negotiations with the intention of reaching a deal before the island's EU accession on 1 May 2004.

A new round of talks got under way the following week in Nicosia. As expected, the process did not go well. Although some progress was made on technical issues, as far as the key constitutional issues were concerned the differences between the two sides remained as deep as ever. Neither leader appeared to want a deal. Denktash, in an apparent effort to derail the negotiations, held frequent press conferences and revealed as much as he could to the media. And though the Greek Cypriots started off with a more constructive approach, by the end they too appeared determined to weaken the process and overloaded the UN with amendments and proposals.

The final chance for a deal now rested on a second round of talks, set to take place in the Swiss mountain resort of Burgenstock, where the two sides would be joined by representatives from Greece and Turkey. But again the talks came to nothing. Denktash boycotted the talks altogether, whereas Papadopoulos went but refused to engage in meaningful negotiations. As a result, and according to the terms of the agreement reached in New York, the UN secretary-general filled in the parts of the plan where no agreement had been reached between the two sides. He submitted what was by now his fifth version of the plan on 31 March. Both communities would then vote on it in a simultaneous referendum to be held just three and a half weeks later, on 24 April.

WHAT DID THE ANNAN PLAN PROPOSE?

In line with the terms of the 1977 and 1979 'high-level agreements', the UN proposals envisaged the establishment of a bizonal, bicommunal federal republic. Specifically, the structure of the state would be based on the Swiss model. There would be a single common state formed by two component states that held political equality. The powers of the component states—as the federal units were called—would consist of anything not directly governed by the common state, and the two component states would cooperate through agreements and constitutional laws that would ensure that they would not infringe upon the functions and powers of each other. Even though the state would have a single international personality, everyone would hold two citizenships—that of the common state and of the component state in which the person resided. There would also be substantial territorial adjustments in favour of the Greek Cypriots, which would take place over a three-year period. Though people would not be entitled to return to their homes, they would be paid compensation based on market values at the time they were lost, adjusted for inflation. Where Greek Cypriots or Turkish Cypriots resided in the component state of the other community they would be given full educational and cultural rights.

As for the political system, the new state would have a parliament made up of two houses—the Senate and the Chamber of Deputies—both of which would have forty-eight members. In the Senate, the two component states would be politically equal at all times and would have twenty-four members each. The relative numbers of seats in the Chamber of Deputies would be determined according to the proportionate population of the two component states, with neither state having less than 25 percent of the seats. Any decisions by the parliament would require a simple majority vote of both houses to pass. There would also be separate legislatures in the two component states and Greek Cypriots and Turkish Cypriots living in the component state of the other community would have the right to be represented in the component state legislature. As for the executive, power would be vested in a six-member presidential council, members of which would be elected by both houses of the parliament from a single list. The offices of president and vice president would rotate among members of the presidential council every ten months. Neither component state (in other words, the Greek and Cypriot communities) would be able to hold the presidency for more than two consecutive terms. However, for the first three years the two current leaders—Papadopoulos and Denktash—would serve as co-presidents. Lastly, a supreme court would also be established that would be made up of nine judges—three Greek Cypriots, three Turkish Cypriots, and three non-Cypriots.

In terms of security and international affairs, the three 1960 treaties—the Treaty of Establishment, the Treaty of Guarantee, and the Treaty of Alliance—would be maintained alongside new treaties with Greece, Turkey, and Britain on matters related to the new situation. As had also been the case under the 1960 constitution, Cyprus would be prohibited from any union with another country, either in whole or in part. At the same time, the island would accede to the European Union and in doing so would henceforth be constitutionally bound to support Turkish EU accession. As required by the EU, it would speak with one voice in all European institutions. In terms of defence, each side would disband its defence forces, and Greece and Turkey would each be permitted to keep up to six thousand troops on the island for seven years, after which the numbers would be gradually reduced with the aim of eventual full withdrawal of all Greek and Turkish forces. Also, the government would not be able to allow any international military operations to take place in Cyprus without the permission of Greece and Turkey. Arms supplies to the country would be banned, and a UN force would also remain on the island to maintain peace alongside a Greek and a Turkish monitoring committee.

WHAT SUPPORT DID THE PROPOSALS RECEIVE?

As soon as the Annan Plan was unveiled, it received widespread support from the United States and most of the members of the European Union. The Turkish government quickly announced that it, too, favoured the proposals. This was an important boost for the pro-settlement camp within the Turkish Cypriot community, which also got to work promoting the benefits of the plan—stressing in particular that the deal would end the isolation of the Turkish Cypriots and that full EU membership as part of a reunified island would lead to a number of significant economic and societal benefits for the community as a whole. However, the plan was also greeted with considerable opposition, both in Turkey and in Cyprus. For example, the nationalist parties in Turkey and parts of the military thought the Annan Plan amounted to a capitulation to the Greek Cypriots and the European Union. Denktash went even further. Vigorously denouncing the plan, he proclaimed that its acceptance would mean nothing less then the end of the Turkish Cypriot community. In the end, the opponents of the proposal were soundly beaten, with 65 percent of Turkish Cypriots voting in favour of the Annan Plan.

The picture on the other side of the Green Line was rather different. Although most Greek Cypriots had been opposed to the agreement since its first unveiling in November 2002, many observers nevertheless hoped that with the support of the two main political parties—AKEL (the communist party) and DISY (the largest centre-right party), which theoretically commanded between 65 and 70 percent of the electorate between them—it might still be possible to win over a majority of Greek Cypriots, especially as the Greek government had also come out in favour of the proposals. It was not to be. The level of opposition was just too high. In an emotional tele-vised address two weeks before the vote, Papadopoulos launched a scathing attack of the UN blueprint and called on the Greek Cypriots to reject it. He argued that another plan could be created that would incorporate all the positions that the Greek Cypriots had long cherished. After his speech, AKEL, a coalition partner in the Papadopoulos administration, decided to back away from its earlier support for the pro-posals. Although DISY came out in favour of the agreement, as did a number of leading political figures, including two former presidents, George Vassiliou and Glafcos Clerides, it was no good. An overwhelming 72 percent of Greek Cypriots voted no. The plan was defeated.

WHY DID THE GREEK CYPRIOTS OPPOSE THE ANNAN PLAN?

Polling suggested that the single most important factor shap-ing the Greek Cypriot decision were concerns over security. Many Greek Cypriots were extremely unhappy with the pro-visions that allowed Turkey to maintain its role as a guarantor power and to keep troops on the island, even if at a drastically reduced level. Others cited a concern over implementation. People wanted to know what assurances existed to make sure that the Turkish government would comply with the terms of the agreement and handed back land and removed troops according to the schedule in the proposals.

Important as these security questions are, they do not begin to present a complete picture of the situation. In fact, in most cases, there was not just a single reason for rejection but a combination of factors. Many people were extremely unhappy at the property provisions; the subject of land is a highly emo-tional subject for the Greek Cypriots. They either did not understand the complicated system of restitution, compensation, and bonds or firmly objected to the fact that they could not get their old land and houses back in entirety. Others were concerned about the viability of the new state and had questions about how the power-sharing structures would work. For some, the worry lay in the economic provisions in the plan. They wanted to know how the new state would manage its finances and what effect reunification would have on key sectors, such as tourism. Another issue was that of the settlers and whether they would be integrated or forced to leave. These were all legitimate concerns.

As in many such situations, some also based their decision on incorrect information. Before the vote all sorts of exaggerated or false claims were made. For instance, it was argued that there was simply no way that anyone could be expected to read through the nine thousand pages of the plan in the few short weeks until the vote. This may have appeared to be a logical concern, until one realises that that the vast majority of these pages were laws that had already been passed by the Greek Cypriot House of Representatives and were already in force as a part of the island's EU accession process. The constitutional aspects of the plan were relatively short. It could be read in a couple of hours by anyone willing to do so. Meanwhile, rumours circulated that the plan could hurt civil servants, with many possibly losing their jobs or being denied pension entitlements. In a country in which almost every family has someone working in the government, this was a serious concern. The government, while not necessarily guilty of circulating such rumours, did nothing to correct them. The Cypriot government even tried to prevent such misinformation from being challenged in the media. Indeed, the state broadcaster decided not to give Alvaro de Soto, the main architect of the Annan Plan, a chance to explain the provisions of the proposals. Likewise, Gunther Verheugen, the EU enlargement commissioner, was also denied an opportunity to explain the European Commission's perspective on various aspects of the plan on state television.

There were also strategic factors at play. For instance, many believed that there was no need to accept the Annan Plan. The island's accession to the European Union would fundamentally alter the balance of power in favour of the Greek Cypriot community. Once in the EU, Cyprus would be in a better position to force Turkey to accept more agreeable terms. A settlement should therefore be resisted until after accession. This view was in many ways encouraged by the decision to hold the referendum just one week before Cyprus was scheduled to join the European Union. Many Greek Cypriots believed that this was evidence of outside powers trying to trick them into accepting a bad solution. Many observers also felt that the decision to vote against the plan was an act of empowerment on the part of some Greek Cypriots. After years of having felt bullied and belittled by Britain and the United States, rejection of the Annan Plan would be their statement of defiance. However, the Turkish media may also have played a part as well. Given the zero-sum thinking that prevails in Cyprus, the fact that the Turkish Cypriots and Turkey were celebrating so much led many Greek Cypriots to conclude that they themselves had received a raw deal. The Turkish government recognised this and called on the Turkish media to temper its enthusiasm. It is unfortunate that they chose to ignore this advice. Last, but not least, there were those who simply did not want a solution—and certainly not on the terms offered in the plan. According to polls released on the night of the vote, 13 percent of Greek Cypriots simply did not want to reunite with the Turkish Cypriots. They believed that it would be better to let the two sides remain as they are.

WHAT WERE THE CONSEQUENCES OF THE VOTE FOR THE TWO SIDES?

Despite predictions that there would be dire consequences if the Greek Cypriots voted against the Annan Plan, in truth the effects were limited. Cyprus was still able to join the European Union just one week after the vote. Where the decision really had an impact was on the standing of the Greek Cypriots in international circles. Having been seen as the more flexible side by most international observers, especially given the intransigent policies adopted by Rauf Denktash, the Greek Cypriots were suddenly seen as the obstacles to peace. Indeed, many previously strong supporters felt betrayed by their behaviour. (Verheugen, the EU enlargement commissioner, said that he felt he had been tricked by the Greek Cypriots.) Within EU diplomatic circles there was a belief that a tacit agreement existed whereby the Greek Cypriots, in return for membership, would accept a viable plan if one was put on the table. Although this was vehemently denied by Papadopoulos, the Republic of Cyprus was nevertheless treated as a pariah by many of its EU partners in the months after accession. It also affected the Greek Cypriots' relationship with the UN. In a report to the Security Council soon after the referendum, Annan heavily criticised Papadopoulos for his behaviour before and during the referendum. Perhaps the most serious consequence was the decision of the Organisation of the Islamic Conference to upgrade the status of the TRNC. But even it stopped short of full recognition.

It was a rather different story for the Turkish Cypriots. There was a widespread belief that the decision of the Turkish

Cypriots to vote in favour of the UN plan would have a very positive effect. In the end, such hopes proved to be illusory. While there was a considerable degree of sympathy for the Turkish Cypriots and a widespread wish to end their isolation, this proved very difficult to do in practice. For instance, international rules and regulations concerning shipping and air traffic made it legally impossible to open Turkish Cypriot ports and airports to direct traffic. In the end, the best that could be achieved was an agreement with the Cypriot government to allow Turkish Cypriot produce to be traded via the ports and airports in the south—the Green Line Regulation. Likewise, efforts by the European Union to provide financial support for a number of major projects in the north was severely hampered by legal questions over property ownership. In real terms the effects of the Turkish Cypriot 'yes' vote were far less wide reaching than many had hoped, and, as a result, the Turkish Cypriots became increasingly bitter, with many believing that they had been deceived by the European Union.

SHOULD A DIVIDED CYPRUS HAVE BEEN ALLOWED TO JOIN THE EUROPEAN UNION?

To answer the question fairly, it is important to look at the situation when the decision to open accession talks with Cyprus was originally taken. At the time, early in the 1990s, the general consensus was that the attempts to find a solution were being hampered by Turkey and the Turkish Cypriot leadership. Under these circumstances, many in the EU felt that it was unfair to penalise the Greek Cypriots for Turkish intransigence or to allow Turkey a right of veto over who could and could not become a member of the union. Likewise, there was a widespread belief that by opening up accession talks with Cyprus the European Union would actually encourage Ankara and Denktash to reconsider their positions and thereby create the conditions for a settlement. Although this view was hotly contested by Turkey, it eventually proved to be correct. The events leading up to the Annan Plan, when Turkey and the Turkish Cypriots played such a constructive role, vindicate this viewpoint. There can be little doubt that had EU membership not be on offer to Cyprus, there would not have been a new peace process in 2002. The decision to allow Cyprus to pursue EU membership was therefore the right one.

But although allowing accession talks was correct, the question of whether Cyprus should actually have been admitted is far more problematic. By the time the referendum took place there was simply no way to reverse the process. From the moment Cyprus signed the Treaty of Accession in Athens in April 2003, its membership was assured. The EU Commission and some member states investigated the option of disentangling Cyprus from the other nine acceding countries, but there was no legal way to do it. It was all or none. Papadopoulos knew this. Moreover, there was nothing the EU could do to make sure that the referendum process was fair or otherwise pressure Papadopoulos until Cyprus was a full member. In this sense, the fault is not so much with the actual decision-making that led to Cypriot membership, but with the European Union's own procedures relating to accession. The Treaty of Accession was signed just weeks after Denktash, not Papadopoulos, had turned down the UN secretary-general's request to put a peace plan to a referendum. It may have been a mistake to admit Cyprus while still divided. However, when judged against the factors at play when it was made, the decision was understandable—even if the outcome has been seen as regrettable by a number of observers.

WHAT WAS THE JULY 2006 AGREEMENT?

In the immediate aftermath of the referendum in 2004 many believed that talks might begin again fairly quickly. If the two sides could sit down at the table, they might be able to hammer out an agreement to amend those areas of the Annan Plan that were considered to be unacceptable the first time around. Some even suggested that there might be another referendum by the end of the year. It didn't happen. Papadopoulos insisted that he would not be rushed into a new peace process. Nor would any future talks be subject to 'stifling timeframes' or international arbitration. In other words, when talks started again, they would be open-ended. This was read by observers to mean that the Greek Cypriot strategy would be to delay the talks for as long as possible, perhaps until Turkey was ready to join the EU. At that point, or so the Greek Cypriot leadership seemed to believe, Ankara, rather than face the prospect of a veto by the Greek Cypriots, would press the Turkish Cypriots to accept a deal on Greek Cypriot terms.

While this may have been the long-term strategy, it soon became obvious that talks could not be delayed for the ten or fifteen years necessary before Turkey would be ready to join the EU. After the initial anger following the referendum subsided, the Greek Cypriot leadership found itself under growing pressure to engage in some form of dialogue with the Turkish Cypriots. On 8 July 2006, the UN managed to broker an agreement between Papadopoulos and Talat on the principles for future talks. These once again reaffirmed that unification would be based on the creation of a bizonal, bicommunal federation with political equality and that a continuation of the status quo was against the interests of both communities. They also agreed to immediate discussions on a range of day-to-day and substantive issues.

At the time, the July 2006 agreement was hailed as an important breakthrough—largely because it was first major statement of joint principles since the 1977 and 1979 high-level agreements. In reality, it amounted to very little. It just opened the way to hold talks about the possibility of reopening discussions. Its relative insignificance was also highlighted by the fact that disputes soon arose over the formation of the teams and the agenda for discussions. Therefore, the agreement proved to be of little practical value.

HOW DID NEW TALKS EMERGE IN 2008?

In the end, it took a change of leadership on the Greek Cypriot side to bring about new talks. In February 2008, the Greek Cypriots went to the polls to elect a new president. In a shock result, Papadopoulos was forced out of the race in the first round. The second-round runoff was won by Dimitris Christofias, the leader of the Cypriot communist party AKEL (Progressive Party of the Working People). Despite having opposed the Annan Plan on tactical grounds in 2004, AKEL and Christofias were generally held to be moderates and during his campaign he had pledged to restart peace talks if he won. True to his word, within weeks of his victory Christofias met with Talat, and the two leaders agreed to restart discussions. In the first phase, it was decided that the talks would be conducted through six working groups covering EU matters, the economy, governance, property, security, and territory.

The hope was that either these groups could resolve a number of matters by themselves or provide guidance to the leaders for later discussion. At the same time, a number of technical committees were set up to explore practical measures for enhanced day-to-day cooperation. The two leaders also decided that the new talks would fall under a Cypriot-led process. Although the UN would facilitate this process—and Alexander Downer, the former Australian foreign minister was appointed as the UN secretary-general's special advisor on Cyprus—it would not act as a mediator.

In September 2008, six months after the working groups and technical committees began meeting, the two leaders agreed to begin regular and direct high-level talks. Again, while it was agreed that this process would be facilitated by the UN, the two sides would remain in control of events. Despite initial optimism that the two leaders, who were believed to have good personal relations, could make significant progress relatively quickly, the talks moved a lot more slowly than many observers hoped or expected. For example, on the question of governance, which was widely felt to be one of the 'easier' areas to tackle, the leaders failed to make much early headway. In large part, this was attributable to the Greek Cypriots' insistence that the Annan Plan could not form the basis for discussions under any circumstances. As a result, many areas where the two sides may have been willing to accept the provisions laid down in the Annan Plan were suddenly thrown open to renegotiation. At the same time, procedural matters got in the way. Greek Cypriot demands that there could be no timetables for the discussions appeared to limit any attempt to quicken the pace of the talks. For their part, the Turkish Cypriots complicated matters by making excessive demands that they knew would be unacceptable to the Greek Cypriots—such as a demand that all mainland Turks be given rights equal to EU citizens in Cyprus, which would include a right to move to the island.

The situation was further complicated when, in April 2010, the Turkish Cypriots voted Talat out of office and elected Dervis Eroglu, a known hard-liner, in his place. Although Eroglu insisted that he would negotiate in good faith, there was little progress between the sides in the months that followed. By the start of 2011, a solution appeared to be as elusive as ever.

4

THE KEY ISSUES

WHAT IS MEANT BY A 'BIZONAL, BICOMMUNAL FEDERATION'?
Since the high-level agreements of 1977 and 1979, the principle of a bizonal, bicommunal federation has been front and centre of efforts to resolve the Cyprus issue. The problem is that a deep difference exists between the two communities as to what the term really means. For the Greek Cypriots, the idea of a bizonal, bicommunal federation refers to a state of affairs whereby a new federation would be created with two federal units, one of which would in all likelihood be predominantly, but not wholly, Greek Cypriot, and the other mainly, but not entirely, Turkish Cypriot. In other words, there would not be a distinct and definitive separation of the two communities. The two states might have features that make them more or less Greek or Turkish Cypriot, but they would not be defined in exclusively ethnic terms.

The Turkish Cypriots have, in contrast, taken a very different view. As they see it, their future survival depends upon their having a piece of territory that is exclusively, or almost exclusively, theirs. In their view, bizonality and bicommunality are intrinsically and inextricably linked. It means that on the one side of the island there would be a Greek Cypriot federal state inhabited almost wholly by Greek Cypriots, and on the other there would be a Turkish Cypriot federal state populated almost entirely by Turkish Cypriots. The numbers of Greek and Turkish Cypriots permitted to live in the 'other' state would be strictly regulated. Any attempt to water this down would inevitably mean that their state would be swamped by Greek Cypriots, who would in time seize hold of the governing structures and thus create two Greek Cypriot federal units. To this extent, while the ideas of bizonality and bicommunality may sound as though they offer a way to reunification, in reality the two communities remain far apart on the practical application of these principles.

WHAT DOES 'POLITICAL EQUALITY' MEAN IN TERMS OF A SOLUTION?

One of the core demands made by the Turkish Cypriots regarding any solution is the requirement that the political equality of the two communities be recognised. In practical terms, this means that any settlement agreed by the two sides must recognise the Turkish Cypriots as fully equal to the Greek Cypriots when it comes to decision making and the governance of the state. The Greek Cypriots cannot have more rights than the Turkish Cypriots simply because they are the majority. Importantly, political equality for the Turkish Cypriots does not mean numerical equality. The Turkish Cypriots recognise that having an equal voice as decision makers within the institutions of state does not mean that they should be allowed equal numbers of personnel in those institutions. For example, while they do expect some sort of right of veto in the decision making procedures, they do not expect to be given 50 percent of the seats in the cabinet or the parliament or half of all posts in government departments.

This would be unrealistic given the difference in size between the two communities. Instead, it is usually accepted that there will be a continuation of the 70:30 balance that was used in the 1960 constitution. The principle of political equality is not considered to be particularly contentious as a concept. The Greek Cypriots have largely, if grudgingly, accepted it. However, what it would mean in real terms, such as division of decision-making responsibilities, is a key question for the sides in negotiations over the type of political system created after a settlement.

WHAT SORT OF FEDERAL SYSTEM AND GOVERNMENTAL STRUCTURE DO THE SIDES WANT?

Disparate views on what the creation of a federation would mean in terms of the ethnic character of the two states is not the only point of disagreement. Sharp divisions also exist over the relationship between the federal states and the central government. The Greek Cypriots insist that the federal institutions be as powerful as possible. As far as they are concerned, as many areas as possible should come under the control of the federal government, with only those areas that are of specific interest to the communities falling under the remit of the administration of the federal units. In contrast, the Turkish Cypriots are determined to make sure that as much power as possible is devolved to the federal units. Wherever possible, the federal states must be able to control their own affairs. Ideally, they would also like to see some elements of foreign affairs and defence come under the control of the communities, such as the right to establish representative offices abroad. In other words, the Greek Cypriots are looking for what is often called a 'tight' federation, whereas the Turkish

Cypriots want to establish a 'loose' federation that comes as close as possible to the concept of a confederation—a subject that will be explored in the next chapter.

On top of all this, there are also a wide range of practical issues that need to be tackled. Again, questions of political equality and the relationship between the federal states and the central government play a very large part in shaping the debate. For example, on the issue of the parliament, questions arise as to whether it should be composed of one house or have an upper and a lower chamber. Most probably, it would be the latter. This means that the relative populations of the two communities would have to be considered. If the upper house (Senate) is made up of an equal number of Greek and Turkish Cypriots, then what would be the proportion in the lower house? Debates have likewise raged about the nature and role of the presidency. Many observers believe that there would have to be some sort of rotating system that would allow the office to be held by Greek and Turkish Cypriots, but on some form of proportional basis. For example, the office would be held by a Greek Cypriot for four years, followed by a Turkish Cypriot for two years. However, suggestions that this was agreed to by Christofias and Talat led to a major backlash by some Greek Cypriot parties and contributed to the decision by EDEK (the socialist party), a junior coalition partner, to leave the government in early 2010. Another suggestion is to form a presidential council that would hold executive authority, with the official role of head of state passing from one member to another throughout its term of office. Finally, questions of law and order need to be addressed. How will policing be managed, and what sort of relationship will exist between the law-and-order mechanisms in the two federal states and between the federal states and the central federal government? Also, the structure of the federal judicial system needs to be addressed, including the representation of the two communities in a supreme court.

WILL THE REPUBLIC OF CYPRUS CONTINUE TO EXIST AFTER A SETTLEMENT?

This is a critically important point. The Turkish Cypriots have often argued that any settlements must be based on the creation of an entirely new state. They assert that the Republic of Cyprus must be dissolved and an entirely new partnership republic must be created between a Greek Cypriot entity, most probably the Greek Cypriot-controlled Republic of Cyprus, and a Turkish Cypriot entity, ideally the Turkish Republic of Northern Cyprus. This is often known as the 'virgin birth model'. The new federal state would be entirely new and would not represent a continuation of any previous state.

The Greek Cypriots strongly reject this idea. As they see it, any settlement must be based on a continuation of the Republic of Cyprus—even if the actual name of the state changes. The reason for this is that the Greek Cypriots believe that the creation of a new federal state by two separate entities could pave the way for eventual secession by the Turkish Cypriots. By accepting that the Turkish Cypriot state was a separate but equal partner in the creation of the new federal state, the Turkish Cypriots could later argue that their state had a right to leave that partnership. In other words, Cyprus could split in the same way that Czechoslovakia did in the early 1990s. The Greek Cypriots, fearful that this is the eventual aim of the Turkish Cypriots, are therefore adamant that any new federal state must represent, in entirety, a formal continuation of the Republic of Cyprus. In this case, any attempt by the Turkish Cypriots to break away would be considered an act of illegal secession. It would also leave the Greek Cypriot leadership in the same situation as they are now, whereby they are recognised as the legitimate and legal government of the state.

WILL THE TERRITORY OF THE STATES CORRESPOND TO THE CURRENT DIVISION OF THE ISLAND?

No. Both sides readily accept that any solution will mean a transfer of territory from the Turkish Cypriots, who currently control 36 percent of the island, to the Greek Cypriots. Usual estimates suggest that the amount returned will be 8–11 percent of the island's total territory. In other words, the size of the Turkish Cypriot entity will be 26–29 percent of the island. But perhaps more important than the question of the amount of territory to be returned to the Greek Cypriots is the question of which areas will be relinquished by the Turkish Cypriots. Linked to territory, one of the key issues for the Greek Cypriots is the question of refugee returns. A central aim for the Greek Cypriot leadership in all the negotiations has been to ensure that as many refugees as possible are able to return to their homes and that as many of those homes as possible be in Greek Cypriot–controlled areas. For this reason, attention has most usually focused on ensuring that the towns of Morphou and Famagusta are returned to Greek Cypriot control. Estimates suggest that the return of these two areas would be sufficient to ensure that the majority of the Greek Cypriots displaced in 1974 would be able to return to their properties and be under Greek Cypriot administration. They are both, therefore, considered to be vital to a settlement.

A more difficult question concerns two other areas: Kyrenia, on the north coast, and the Karpas Peninsula, the famous

Cyprus panhandle that juts out to the east of the island. By almost all reckoning, Kyrenia will not be returned to Greek Cypriot control. Even though it had the largest proportion of Greek Cypriots of all the major towns on the island prior to the invasion (there were more Greeks in Kyrenia as a percentage of the entire population than in Nicosia, Limassol, Larnaca, or Famagusta), it is right in the middle of Turkish Cypriot–controlled territory. It is therefore extremely difficult to see how the Turkish Cypriots would ever be willing to give it up. Another question relates to the Karpas Peninsula, which was also largely inhabited by Greek Cypriots prior to 1974, and still has a very small community of enclaved Greek Cypriots living there. This is perhaps easier to address inasmuch as it remains fairly sparsely populated and is not seen as central to the creation of a geographically viable Turkish Cypriot federal unit. It is therefore quite conceivable that it could be returned to Greek Cypriot control or made into some form of federal holding. However, this would almost certainly require tradeoffs elsewhere, as giving up the peninsula would mean that the size of the Turkish Cypriot state would probably be less than 26 percent of the island.

HOW WILL PROPERTY ISSUES BE ADDRESSED?

Although a territorial readjustment would allow many Greek Cypriots to return to their properties, questions would remain concerning Greek Cypriot properties in areas that remain under Turkish Cypriot control. This is an extremely contentious issue. It is, along with security, the most important issue for Greek Cypriots in any settlement. Unsurprisingly, the two communities have rather different ways of addressing the problem. Whereas the Greek Cypriots have traditionally argued that all displaced persons should have their entire property returned to them, the Turkish Cypriots have tended to call for some form of property exchange. This would allow Turkish Cypriot properties in the south to be swapped for Greek Cypriot properties in the north. (Or, at least, swap those properties belonging to Turkish Cypriot owners who have no desire to return and live in the south.) Some form of compensation could then make up the difference.

Both ideas have flaws, and each is considered unacceptable by the other side. For instance, the Turkish Cypriots argue that returning all Greek Cypriot property to its original owners would make it impossible to create a Turkish Cypriot federal unit. If all the Greek Cypriots who had property in the north were to return, they would radically outnumber the Turkish Cypriots. In contrast, the Greek Cypriots see any attempt to deprive people of their land as an infringement of their human rights. Also, by trying to prevent Greek Cypriots from returning to their homes, the Turkish Cypriots are attempting to create ethnically homogenous areas, thereby perpetuating the division of the island and contravening fundamental EU principles on freedom of movement and the right to settle within the union. To this extent, the Greek Cypriot position is that most, if not all, Greek Cypriots must be given the right to return to their homes if they so wish.

Under the terms of the Annan Plan, the question was addressed by a complex system that used three mechanisms to navigate a path between the two positions. In essence, the plan proposed that all Greek and Turkish Cypriots have one-third of their property returned to them. They would then receive compensation for one-third, which each community would pay to its own members. Finally, tradable bonds would be issued to cover eventual compensation for the final third.

(Subsequent studies have showed that these bonds could have become very valuable.) At the same time, controls would be introduced that restricted people from returning to live in their properties full time. In many cases, people would be allowed only to visit their homes for a certain number of nights a week, on a transitional basis. The proposals were not popular. Most Greek Cypriots resented the fact that they could not have all of their property and were subject to restrictions. They objected to the requirement that the Greek Cypriot administration would have to compensate Greek Cypriots for land taken and occupied by Turkey and the Turkish Cypriots. Finally, the idea of the bonds was poorly understood and was viewed with deep suspicion. In all likelihood, resolving the issue will require fairly substantial compromises and a mixture of return, exchange, and compensation.

WILL THERE BE FREEDOM OF MOVEMENT AND SETTLEMENT ACROSS THE ISLAND?

At one time, the question of the freedom of movement was highly contentious. Throughout the 1980s and 1990s, when the Turkish Cypriot administration under Rauf Denktash imposed harsh restrictions on crossings between the two sides, the Greek Cypriots insisted that any fair and viable settlement would ensure that all Cypriots had the right to move freely around the island with no restrictions based on ethnicity. However, the debate over the freedom of movement has now ended. Since the opening of the Green Line in April 2003, Greek and Turkish Cypriots have been free to come and go across the dividing line, and it seems very hard to imagine that this will change after a settlement.

While the freedom of movement is now accepted by both sides, freedom of settlement remains highly controversial. Once again, it relates closely to the question of bizonality and bicommunality. For the Greek Cypriots, the right to live where one wants is extremely important and should not be subject to limitations. The Turkish Cypriots, on the other hand, want some restrictions. It is one thing to allow everyone to move freely around the island. It is something quite different to allow people to settle at will where they want; it could well lead to large numbers of Greek Cypriots moving into the Turkish Cypriot federal state.

The Annan Plan contained provisions limiting the number of Greek and Turkish Cypriots able to settle in the two constituent states. This was a deeply unpopular measure among Greek Cypriots, even though it was suggested by some observers that the provisions would almost certainly have meant that any Greek Cypriot who wanted to return home could do so. After all, few Greek Cypriots refugees appeared to want to give up their new lives, jobs, and friends to return to homes that they had left almost forty years previously. Moreover, their children, who had never lived in the north, would be even less inclined to do so. But it was the principle that mattered. Many Greek Cypriots fundamentally object to the idea of any restriction on the right of people to settle. Even though it seems likely that even fewer Greek Cypriots would now want to return to the north in the event of a settlement, many Greek Cypriots believe that the principle of the freedom of settlement is as important as the practical application of that right. It is therefore likely that the issue of freedom of settlement will continue to play a major role in discussions.

WILL ALL TURKISH SETTLERS HAVE TO LEAVE THE ISLAND?

The question of Turkish settlers is highly charged. Over the years, Greek Cypriots have insisted that a fair and viable solution to the Cyprus Problem would be based on the repatriation of all Turkish troops and all Turkish settlers. They argue, with good reason, that the decision by Turkey to introduce large numbers of settlers represents a deliberate attempt by the Turkish government to change the demographic situation on the island. This is a serious allegation inasmuch as attempts to change the facts on the ground by colonising occupied territory amounts to a war crime according to the 1949 Fourth Geneva Convention and the 1977 additional protocol to the convention.

In reality, however, the expulsion of all the Turkish settlers will not happen. First of all, not all Turkish citizens now living in Cyprus can be regarded as settlers. Many have married Turkish Cypriots and thus have a legitimate right to live on the island. Second, it has now been more than thirty-five years since the invasion, which means that many of the children of the original settlers brought to the island in the immediate aftermath of the invasion are now approaching middle age and have children of their own who were born and raised on the island. Cyprus, not Turkey, is their home. Strict adherence to a demand that they all be deported would mean that tens of thousands of people would be forced to live in a country they do not know. The question of the settlers is therefore no longer strictly a legal question; it is also a humanitarian issue. Under the Annan Plan, forty thousand Turkish citizens living in Cyprus who had been granted TRNC citizenship would have been permitted to remain on the island. Although this was not popular among Greek Cypriots, many nevertheless recognise the human dimension of the issue. It therefore seems certain that in any future settlement process the question will not be about whether all Turkish settlers should go home, but how many should be permitted to stay and according to what criteria. Indeed, in the latest talks, Christofias is reported to have agreed that fifty thousand could stay.

WILL THE TREATIES OF GUARANTEE AND ALLIANCE CONTINUE?

Security remains a key consideration for both communities in any settlement process. It is also the area where, on the face of it, there is least room for agreement between the two sides given that their starting positions are diametrically opposed to one another. The Greek Cypriots adamantly oppose the continuation of the Treaty of Guarantee and the Treaty of Alliance. As far as they are concerned, it is wholly unacceptable that the constitutional structure of the Cypriot state should be subject to the guarantee of any third countries, let alone that these states also have a right to intervene militarily. Such an idea is contrary to the very principles of state sovereignty and has no place in the twenty-first century, especially as they relate to a state that is a member of the European Union. Likewise, permanently stationing Turkish troops on the island, especially when linked with a right of intervention, represents a fundamental threat to the security and stability of the Cypriot state. All Turkish troops must therefore be removed.

The Turkish Cypriots and Turkey take a very different view. As far as they are concerned there can be no changes to either the Treaty of Guarantee or the Treaty of Alliance. They argue that past experience has shown that the Greek Cypriots cannot be trusted. Unless Turkey has a right to intervene, there can be no guarantees that the Greek Cypriots will abide by the terms of any settlement. Additionally, the presence of Turkish military forces, backed up by a legal right of intervention, offers the best safeguards that the Turkish Cypriots will be protected from attack. Therefore, while the number of troops present after a settlement is open to negotiation, they cannot be removed altogether.

Finding a solution to this issue will not be easy. However, there are ideas. One suggestion that received attention at the time of the Annan Plan was for the introduction of a 'sunset clause' on the Treaty of Guarantee dictating that the treaty continue until Turkey joined the European Union or until a certain period of time had elapsed, after which the treaty would dissolve. Likewise, although the Greek Cypriots have taken a strong stand against the continued presence of Turkish troops on the island, many in the international community suspect that they would be prepared to accept a certain number provided that the troops would remain on the island for a very limited period of time and that, from the moment an agreement is reached, their number was reduced significantly. While finding a solution to the question of security will not be easy, there are nevertheless options that might well, with the right circumstances and good will, lead to a mutually acceptable compromise.

WHAT ASSURANCES WILL EXIST THAT AN AGREEMENT BE IMPLEMENTED?

Another major Greek Cypriot concern that will need to be addressed in any future settlement effort is the question of implementation. Many Greek Cypriots remain deeply distrustful of Turkey and do not believe that it will be willing to uphold its side of any agreement. They want to know how the international community, including the European Union and the UN Security Council, will ensure that any deal reached will be upheld fully by both sides. This is especially important to the Greek Cypriots as it is likely that the provisions of an agreement that will be phased in will apply to the Turkish Cypriots, whereas their concessions will be made immediately—as was the case under the Annan Plan. For example, any new constitutional structure to the state will be put in place from the start. At the moment a settlement comes into force, the Greek Cypriots will be expected to share power fully with the Turkish Cypriots. However, the Turkish Cypriots will not be expected to hand back all land and properties to Greek Cypriots immediately because new homes will have to be built first for the displaced Turkish Cypriots. Likewise, Turkish troops cannot be expected to leave at the moment a new arrangement comes into force. It will take time to redeploy them. All this creates the real potential for delays and postponements, and it is this that the Greek Cypriots are determined to avoid.

What this means in real terms is hard to say. Most observers expect that the Security Council will pass a resolution emphasising the importance of abiding by the terms of an agreement (assuming, of course, that the Greek Cypriot leaders do not try to prevent such a measure from being passed, as Papadopoulos did in 2004). But the effect of this is likely to be more moral than practical. It seems highly unlikely that formal sanctions would be placed on Turkey for noncompliance. There will certainly not be military action to force Turkey to remove its troops in the event that it fails to meet the terms of a withdrawal. Instead, the most likely response would be a call for further talks and negotiations. This worries the Greek Cypriots, who feel that under such circumstances they would inevitably be asked to make concessions on timetables and show flexibility and understanding. Likewise, it seems highly unlikely that the European Union would be willing to take strong action against Turkey. Having said this, it does have some power to shape the process. For example, the EU could issue a declaration stating that Turkey's accession course is linked to its willingness to implement an agreement.

WILL BRITAIN HAVE TO GIVE UP ITS MILITARY BASES AS PART OF A SETTLEMENT?

No, not formally. Even the Greek Cypriots, who have long expressed a hope that the British Sovereign Base Areas would eventually cease to exist, have made clear that they do not see a discussion over the bases as being an integral part of the settlement effort. Instead, the general view and the official position of President Christofias is that the issue should be opened only once a settlement has been reached. As Christofias has explained, there is nothing to be gained by opening up a second front with Britain at a time when the primary focus of attention must be on reaching an agreement with Turkey and the Turkish Cypriots. A settlement will nonetheless almost certainly lead to some major changes. In 2004, Britain explicitly stated that it would be willing to relinquish part of the base areas if the two sides agreed to a settlement, and in late 2009 the British government confirmed that the offer would stand in the event of a peace deal.

WHAT WILL BE THE RELATIONSHIP BETWEEN CYPRUS AND THE EU?

While it may not seem to be the most important of issues, the question of how Cyprus will interact with the European Union following a settlement is very important. This explains why the sides agreed to establish a working group on EU matters when talks resumed in 2008. At this stage, there is no question about Cyprus's continued membership in the European Union. However, serious questions exist over how decisions will be taken on EU matters and how Cyprus will be represented in EU institutions, such as the European Commission and the European Parliament. This issue is mostly related to federalism and the relationship between the federal states in a post-settlement Cyprus. The Greek Cypriots would like to ensure that on all EU related matters, the island speaks with one voice and has a single representation. The Turkish Cypriots would rather see separate representation on certain matters. For its part, the European Union would seem to be far closer to the Greek Cypriot position, arguing that Cyprus must be represented in a unified manner within EU institutions and must speak with a single voice on all key issues.

HOW WILL THE ECONOMIC ASPECTS OF A SOLUTION BE MANAGED?

While attention is usually focused on the issues of territory, property, governance, and security, there are a number of other matters that will also need to be agreed between the two sides. For example, questions relating to the efficient management of the economy will need to be tackled. By no means simple or straightforward, regulation of the economy touches upon almost all aspects of the settlement. For example, questions regarding revenue raising and expenditure have important implications for the nature of the relationship between the federal government and the federal states. There is also the question of the administration of monetary policy. While this second question has, to a certain extent, been addressed by the accession of Cyprus to the European Union and the adoption of the euro, there are still areas in which national governments do have a direct say that will need to be tackled.

On another note, serious questions exist with regard to the cost of reunification and reconstruction. How will compensation for people who have lost their homes be funded? What sort of international grants and aid will be made available to ensure a rapid convergence between the economies of the two federal units? And how will construction and renovation costs be managed? Having been fenced off for almost forty years, many of the building in Varosha, for example, will have to be demolished and rebuilt. Indeed, the question of how a settlement will be paid for is a very real concern.

So too is the question of the economic disparity between the two communities. Many Turkish Cypriots fear that in the aftermath of reunification, the wealthier Greek Cypriots will take control of the economy of the north, thereby undermining the political settlement. Suggestions have been made that there should be some limitation on the free movement of capital following a solution. The problem is that this could undermine the economic development of the north, which would ensure that the Greek Cypriots have to bear a disproportionate responsibility for funding the central administration for longer. This in turn could then perpetuate tensions between the two communities as the Greek Cypriots would feel that they are bankrolling an agreement that limits their rights. These are all serious economic and financial issues that were raised during the debates on the Annan Plan and will arise again in any future discussions on reunification.

5

CURRENT AND FUTURE SETTLEMENT EFFORTS

WILL THE UN RETAIN RESPONSIBILITY FOR PEACEMAKING AND PEACEKEEPING?

Following the failure of the Annan Plan and the accession of Cyprus to the European Union, some Greek Cypriots argued that the UN should cease to be responsible for finding a solution. The EU should take over instead. This is unlikely to happen. For a start, the Turkish Cypriots would never accept it. With the Greek Cypriot–controlled government of Cyprus now a full member of the union, few believe that the EU could be an impartial mediator. Perhaps more important, the EU itself is opposed to the idea. Both within the commission and among the member states is a strong belief that the ultimate responsibility for peacemaking should remain in the hands of the UN. This has also been the position of other relevant actors, such as the United States and the Russian Federation. Looking ahead, it seems likely that the UN will continue to play the central role in the search for a solution for the foreseeable future.

As for the task of peacekeeping, there is a generally held belief that this will also continue to come under the purview of the United Nations. But quite what this will mean in real terms is less certain. Following the failure of the Annan Plan, there were discussions about the future of the UN Force in Cyprus and it was even suggested that it be downgraded from a full peacekeeping force of approximately a thousand troops to an observer mission of less than a hundred personnel. This idea was rejected in favour of a reduction to the current 860 peacekeepers, but questions continue about whether the ongoing international presence on the island can be justified indefinitely. Although the cost of the force is relatively low (in 2009, the budget of the force was US $56.9 million), and a third of the money comes from the governments of Cyprus and Greece, many observers nevertheless feel that the UN's resources could be better deployed elsewhere. There is also a feeling that peacekeeping should be undertaken to enable a settlement and should not be a permanent undertaking in its own right. It therefore seems likely that unless a settlement is reached, there will be further calls for the presence of the force to be reviewed with a view to a reduction in its size or possible withdrawal altogether.

In the event of an agreement, it also seems likely that the UN will remain the main peacekeeping force. Although other options, such as NATO or the EU, have been suggested as alternatives, the first is likely to be opposed by the Greek Cypriots and the second by Turkey. As for the size and role of the post-settlement mission, this will be determined at the time of an agreement. But it would seem likely that there would be an increase in the size of the peacekeeping mission in the immediate aftermath of an agreement, but that it would then be reduced—or even removed entirely—as the situation settles down.

WHAT PART DOES THE UN SECURITY COUNCIL PLAY IN SETTLEMENT EFFORTS?

The UN Security Council plays a large part in settlement efforts. The council is vested with ultimate authority to oversee both the peacemaking and peacekeeping activities in Cyprus. For instance, the mandate for the UN Force in Cyprus is subject to renewal by the Security Council every six months, a process that requires a full report from the UN secretary-general.

At the same time, the five permanent members of the Security Council—Britain, China, France, Russia, and the United States—also play, or have the potential to play, a large part in efforts to find a solution. Of these five, perhaps the most significant is Britain. By virtue of its constitutional role as a guarantor power it is closely involved in settlement efforts. The United States inevitably plays a major role as well. In fact, since the early 1960s, albeit with certain exceptions, there has been a tendency by Britain and the United States to work closely with one another on matters relating to Cyprus. This has given rise to conspiracy theories, such as those associated with 1974, and led to accusations that Britain and the United States are scheming to prevent reunification or to achieve it on terms that overwhelmingly favour Turkey and the Turkish Cypriots. However, it appears that the process in 2004 has left its mark on the way in which both Britain and the United States deal with Cyprus. In line with the United Nation's insistence that the talks which started in 2008 are primarily in the hands of the Cypriot communities, London and Washington have had little direct influence on the negotiations. Both have sought to emphasise the Cypriot nature of the process.

Another important actor is Russia. Although it has not been as prominent in the Cyprus issue as Britain or the United States, it has nevertheless played a role in developments over the years. For example, in 1964, it was Soviet involvement that prevented the establishment of a NATO-based peacekeeping force on the island. More recently, in 2004, Moscow vetoed a proposed Security Council resolution that would have provided certain security guarantees designed to underpin the Annan Plan. (Although the Greek Cypriots denied that this move was made at their behest, the weight of evidence suggests otherwise.) Likewise, after the failure of the Annan Plan, Russia was instrumental in preventing a reduction in the size of the UN peacekeeping force—a move that the Greek Cypriots had opposed. In this sense, Russia is seen by the Greek Cypriots as protecting their interests in the Security Council. In return, Cyprus is a small but important pro-Russian voice in the European Union.

As for France and China, neither has traditionally taken much interest in Cyprus. Paris has tended to view Cyprus as a former British colony and a member of the Commonwealth and therefore as a British issue. Although this appeared to be changing after 2004, when the Papadopoulos administration sought French support as a means of counteracting British influence in the EU, it seems unlikely that France will take a major role in the future. China, on the other hand, may well become more active in the years ahead. After having long ignored events outside of its immediate sphere of influence, Beijing in recent years has become increasingly interested in international events more generally. What this might mean in real terms is hard to say, but given China's strong support for principles of sovereignty and territorial integrity, it likely will come out on the Greek Cypriot side.

WHAT IS THE 'EUROPEAN SOLUTION' TO THE CYPRUS PROBLEM?

From time to time, Greek Cypriots refer to the need to find a European Solution to the Cyprus Problem. Many outsiders assume this refers to a moderate and forward-looking proposal for a settlement. In fact, the term 'European Solution' refers to a particular settlement model favoured by nationalists within the Greek Cypriot community. Before the Annan Plan was proposed, the view emerged that if a settlement could be delayed until after the island joined the European Union, new circumstances would arise that would ensure a solution more favourable to the Greek Cypriot community. First of all, the EU would ensure that democracy would be implemented on the basis of one person, one vote. This would give the Greek Cypriots, as the majority, overall political control of the island's administration. Second, it would ensure the full and fair implementation of human rights, which they read as the full return of all property expropriated by the Turkish state. Third, there would be no derogations from the *acquis communautaire*, the EU's body of laws. This would mean that the fundamental principles of the European Union, including the right of freedom of settlement, would be fully applied, thereby preventing the creation of an ethnically Turkish Cypriot federal state. In other words, despite its positive sounding name, the European Solution represented the abandonment of the creation of a bizonal, bicommunal republic and the establishment of a Greek Cypriot–controlled unitary state.

Of course, each of the points was based either on a misreading or misrepresentation of how the European Union works. First, nowhere in the union is democracy equated with full proportionality. Indeed, this principle is rarely found in political systems. For example, in the U.S. Senate, all states are equally represented, despite the massive population disparities between, say, California and Rhode Island. Second, the idea that all property must be returned to its owners, with no exceptions, is not fully supported by the law. There is not an automatic right to own property under any and all circumstances. In some cases, property must be expropriated for the public good—for example, to build a highway. Rather, international law recognises that people cannot be arbitrarily deprived of their property. There must be some fair and legitimate process. In the case of Cyprus, there is an argument to be made that in some cases the expropriation of property, with appropriate compensation, may have to be accepted in order to enable a settlement, which one could argue is the ultimate public good. Third, there is nothing to say that all EU laws must be universally applied at all times, with no exceptions. While there is an innate preference within the EU for the equal application of principles and legislation across all member states, it is also recognised that exceptions can and should be made under certain circumstances. In the case of Cyprus, while it is hoped that the freedom of settlement will eventually be applied, most observers recognise that there will need to be some sort of transition period.

HAS EU ACCESSION CHANGED THE PARAMETERS OF A SOLUTION?

Although advocates of a European Solution argue that the island's accession to the European Union has opened the way for a radical change in the parameters of a settlement, the effects of accession on the search for a solution have been modest. Apart from the introduction of a working group on EU issues and changes in the way economic issues are tackled, the ideas under discussions now appear much the same as they were before Cyprus joined the EU. The ways in which governance, property, territory, and security are being addressed seem to be relatively unchanged, in large part because the EU does not govern the internal political structures of its member states. However, a number of important issues do need to be discussed through the prism of the EU inasmuch as exceptions (derogations) to the *acquis communautaire* might be needed. For example, any decisions to limit the freedom of settlement will need to have EU endorsement as freedom of movement—defined in this context as a right to live and work throughout the 27 member states—is a fundamental principle of the union.

The influence of the EU can also be felt in more subtle ways. For instance, at a technical level, there is the question of Turkish Cypriot adaptation to the terms of the *acquis communautaire*. This is a fundamental requirement under any settlement. This means that most of the legislation that would need to be harmonised between the two sides following a settlement would have to be based on laws already passed by the Greek Cypriots as a result of their membership of the Union. (Although work is being done to try to ensure that the Turkish Cypriots also adapt their legislation to meet EU requirements, this is insufficiently developed at this stage.) Similarly, the adoption of the euro as the official currency of the Republic of Cyprus and the consequences of this for economic policy would need to be taken into account in any settlement process.

IS A SETTLEMENT LINKED TO TURKEY'S EU MEMBERSHIP?

Conventional wisdom suggests that a solution will come about only if Turkey receives a clear promise of EU membership. Otherwise, the thinking goes, there will simply be no incentive for Ankara to withdraw its forces from the island and put pressure on the Turkish Cypriots to play a constructive part in securing an agreement with the Greek Cypriots. Those who defend this view often note that Turkish support for the Annan Plan was directly linked to its wish for EU membership.

While such thinking was, until recently, the standard view of the situation—no EU membership, no solution—there are signs that things may be changing. A far more interesting picture is emerging that sees a link between Turkey's EU membership and a Cyprus solution but does not make one dependent upon the other. In recent years, Turkey has sought to increase its profile on the world stage. To do this, the Turkish government has actively pursued a policy of détente with its neighbours—the 'Zero Problems' policy. Over the past decade, Turkey has made efforts to repair or improve relations with Greece, Iran, Iraq, and Syria. More recently, steps have even been taken to address the long-standing animosity between Turkey and Armenia. Cyprus remains the last major issue to be tackled. Once it is out of the way, then Turkey can concentrate on consolidating its reputation as a regional leader and a major international actor. This in turn could make Turkey more attractive as a prospective member of the EU. In this sense, while many in Turkey—including important elements within the military and foreign policy establishment—still believe that a solution to the Cyprus Problem should depend on EU accession, many others believe that resolving the issue would be beneficial for Turkey in a far wider sense.

WHAT ROLE DOES GREECE PLAY IN SETTLEMENT EFFORTS?
Unlike Ankara, Athens is not in a position to shape the negotiating position of the Greek Cypriots. Since 1974, following the

Greek military coup and the Turkish invasion, successive Greek governments have accepted the formula that Nicosia decides and Athens follows. In other words, Greece does not try to dictate the terms of a settlement to the Greek Cypriots but respects the decisions that they reach. This does not, of course, mean that Athens and Nicosia are in complete agreement at all times. For instance, in 2004, the Greek government came out in favour of the Annan Plan, despite strong objections to the proposals from the Greek Cypriot leadership. More recently, there have been signals that Greece has decided to distance itself from Cyprus. Following Cypriot accession to the European Union, which came about as a result of strong Greek lobbying, it would appear as if Greek government is content to let Cyprus fight its own battles. Several times, for example, the Cypriot government sought to take a hard line on Turkish EU accession but found no support from Greece. This is not to say that the links between Greece and Cyprus have disappeared. Greek Cypriot leaders still consult closely and regularly with the Greek government. However, Greece has very little influence over Greek Cypriot decisions.

CAN THE CURRENT STATUS QUO CONTINUE INDEFINITELY?

In the absence of any prospect for a settlement, the question frequently arises as to whether the continuation of the status quo is perhaps the best outcome. The current situation can continue indefinitely. After all, there is no conflict on the island. However, it should also be recognised that as time passes the present stalemate is likely to become less and less appealing for both sides. First, as Turkey seeks to move closer to the European Union and consolidate its position on the world stage, it is ever more apparent that Cyprus represents an ongoing obstacle to these ambitions. Second, the increase in the number of lawsuits brought by Greek Cypriot property owners for loss of the use of their property is likely to become ever more costly for Turkey, which will have to compensate the owners or face the legal, political, and financial consequences of failing to do so—a situation reaffirmed by the European Court of Human Rights in early 2010. Worse, a major court case—the Orams case—has opened the way for claims for compensation to be made in the courts in the south against anyone occupying Greek Cypriot properties in the north. More important, now that Cyprus is a member of the EU, these judgements can be enforced across the entire European Union. Looking ahead, this form of 'lawfare', as it has been called, is likely to get even worse. Even ordinary tourists to the north could start to face fines for staying in hotels, or even eating at restaurants, that are built on Greek Cypriot land. Such a scenario is not unrealistic. The Greek Cypriot lawyer who won the Orams case has already said that a case against tourists will be his next target. If this succeeds, it could have a catastrophic effect on the Turkish Cypriot economy, which is already reeling after the collapse in property prices. To this extent, it is clear that the current status quo is not in the interests of either Turkey or the Turkish Cypriots.

It is not just the north that needs a solution. The Greek Cypriots are also likely to face significant problems if the current status quo continues. Most important, the long-standing Greek Cypriot belief that the law is on their side and that they can wait until a better set of circumstances for a settlement has not been borne out. In a landmark ruling delivered in early 2010, the European Court of Human Rights noted that the passage of time is changing the situation on the ground in the north, and that this must be taken into account when considering the question of property restitution. Moreover, with every passing year, the number of Turkish settlers in the north increases. This is already having a profound effect on the Turkish Cypriot community, which is well on its way to becoming a minority to the mainland Turkish settlers. For the Greek Cypriots it means that if a solution does occur, they will not be uniting with the Turkish Cypriots, but with a predominantly Turkish entity in the north. The bonds of common heritage and shared culture—what little effect that it might have—will not be there at all. This will make cooperation in a postconflict Cyprus significantly more difficult. But even at a day-to-day level, the effects of the division are being felt more acutely. Since the opening of the Green Line in April 2003, many Turkish Cypriots have made use of the benefits of their Cypriot citizenship to claim various benefits, such as free hospital treatment, from the Cypriot state. This is on top of the gains, such as freedom of movement around Europe, they have made since Cyprus joined the EU. However, they are not taxpayers. This has led to resentment among many Greek Cypriots and to comments from at least one prominent Greek Cypriot political figure suggesting that perhaps partition would be the most logical and desirable outcome (something that will be explored a little later on). Such sentiments will only increase if, as some have suggested, the Turkish Cypriots start to move into the south and claim their political rights under the 1960 constitution. If this happens— and it should be stressed that it is unlikely; the more probable outcome is that Turkish Cypriots will just choose to move elsewhere in the EU, most probably Britain or Germany—the Greek Cypriots could well be left with a Turkish entity on one side of the line and a mixed Greek Cypriot–Turkish Cypriot state on the other. In other words, they will not only have lost the north, they will also have lost their absolute control over the south as well.

WILL FUTURE SETTLEMENT EFFORTS BE BASED ON A FEDERAL SOLUTION?

For all the reasons listed above, the continuation of the status quo appears to be increasingly unviable. There is a clear imperative for the two sides to reach an agreement. The question is what type of settlement they could reach. At the moment, it seems probable that the search for a solution will continue to be based on trying to establish a bizonal, bicommunal federation—if only because the sides disagree far more on the alternative options. Polls have consistently shown that neither the Greek Cypriots nor the Turkish Cypriots place a federation at the top of their list of desired options for a solution. The most favoured result for the Greek Cypriots would be, as noted earlier, the creation of a unitary state in which the Turkish Cypriots have strong minority rights but where political power lies firmly in the hands of the majority Greek Cypriot population. The second-best would be a federal settlement, followed by a confederation and then partition. For the Turkish Cypriots, the most desirable outcome would be either a confederation or a formalised division of the island. A federation comes next, with very few, if any, willing to accept a unitary state. In this sense, the proposals for a federation bridge the gap between the desirable and the feasible for both communities. Although neither side seems particularly enamoured with the idea, it nevertheless remains the most acceptable compromise solution and is therefore likely to remain on the table as the basis for discussions.

COULD A SOLUTION BE BASED ON A CONFEDERATION
OR A UNITARY STATE?

If it is not possible to negotiate the creation of a federation, what other options are available? The first two ideas to consider are confederation or the establishment of a unitary state. Most Turkish Cypriots would prefer the former model, in which the two states would enter into a voluntary association whereby almost all powers would be located within the Greek and Turkish Cypriot entities. There would be a minimal role for the central government, covering just foreign affairs and some defence and economic competencies. However, the idea has been roundly rejected by the Greek Cypriots for two main reasons. First of all, they are reluctant to agree to a solution that merely perpetuates the current situation. Many Greek Cypriots believe that Turkish Cypriot demands for a confederation are meant to ensure that in return for some land, the Turkish Cypriots will simply be allowed to continue on as before, with only a minimal degree of contact between the two communities. Such a model would even allow the Turkish Cypriots to have considerable control over aspects of foreign or even defence affairs. Second, there is a deep concern that a confederation would simply pave the way for a formal split at a later stage. Crudely put, the difference between a federation and a confederation is that in the former, power flows from the central state to the federal units. In a confederation, this is reversed. The central government has only those powers that are given to it by the states. For this reason, many Greek Cypriots believe that the Turkish Cypriots prefer a confederation because they believe that as soon as any problems emerge they can call a referendum and separate, in rather the same way as the Czech Republic and Slovakia or Serbia and Montenegro separated.

Equally, opinion polls have consistently shown that the preferred solution for most Greek Cypriots is the creation of a unitary state in which the Turkish Cypriots would have strong minority rights but not political equality with the Greek Cypriots. In other words, this would see a continuation of the 1960 constitution, but amended in such a way that that the reintegration of the Turkish Cypriots would cause as little political disruption as possible. Obviously, this is a wholly unacceptable option for the Turkish Cypriots. The idea that they would be willing to reintegrate back into the Republic of Cyprus, but instead of having the powers granted to them in 1960 they would accept some sort of minority rights, is completely unrealistic. Almost all Turkish Cypriots would prefer to maintain the current situation, or even unite with Turkey, than accept this as a solution. Granted, such a system need not be a disaster for the community. The EU does ensure strong minority rights. Also, this form of integration would open the way for the Turkish Cypriots to have full access to all the benefits of EU membership. However, it would mean having to give up any claim to a defined and secure Turkish Cypriot territory in Cyprus. Even with the safeguards provided by the European Union, this idea seems unlikely to ever be accepted. Turkish Cypriots view the creation of a unitary state as the beginning of the end of their community.

While neither option is on the table at the moment, it seems almost certain that of the two, the formation of a confederation is the more likely alternative in the future. Many Greek Cypriots believe that things have been heading in this direction anyway. The Annan Plan was widely seen to lay the foundations for a weak federation. At some point, the line may be crossed. In contrast, it seems all but certain that a unitary state will not come about.

ARE ENOSIS OR TAKSIM STILL POSSIBLE OPTIONS?

While nationalist Turkish Cypriots will often argue that enosis remains a real dream for the Greek Cypriots, this is not the case. For the Greek Cypriots, enosis simply does not exist as an option under any settlement formula. After fifty years of independence, Greek Cypriots are now content with the Republic of Cyprus. They would not want to give up the Cypriot state to become a province of Greece, thereby losing their independent voice in the United Nations and the European Union.

In contrast, the possibility that the north might one day be annexed by Turkey cannot be so easily dismissed. But it is not a widely held wish among Turkish Cypriots. Instead, it is more a product of changing circumstances. Polls have shown that ideally the Turkish Cypriots would like to have their own state. However, if this cannot happen, the next-best options would be a confederation or a federation. If both of these scenarios prove impossible to achieve, then at some point a question might have to be asked about the possibility of unification between the north and Turkey. This has been explicitly raised as an option on a number of occasions, such as the threat in 2001 by the Turkish government to annex the north. While it seems unlikely that this option, which would undoubtedly cause severe damage to Turkey's relationship with the European Union, would be favoured by the current government in Ankara, this is not to say that it might not arise as an option in the future—especially if Turkey's path to EU membership comes to an end. Such a scenario is all the more likely given the demographic changes in the north. The settlers, either first or second generation, have a greater sense of affiliation with Turkey than do the Turkish Cypriots. (Having said this, evidence suggests that children of the settlers adapt to Turkish

Cypriot values very quickly.) They do not fear the prospect of greater integration with, or even annexation by, Turkey.

COULD THE TRNC BE RECOGNISED?

Another option would be for the Turkish Republic of Northern Cyprus to be recognised as a sovereign and independent state, thereby forcing the Greek Cypriots to accept the reality on the ground. While Kosovo's unilateral declaration of independence in 2008 increased speculation that this could happen, it is very unlikely that many states would recognise the TRNC. For a start, there is an explicit UN resolution prohibiting recognition. Recognition would therefore be clearly contrary to international law, and it seems very unlikely that this resolution will be rescinded. Even if the United States were to support recognition, and there is no evidence to suggest that it would, the other permanent members of the Security Council would not. Quite apart from the problems Britain and France would face in terms of recognising the forced division of a fellow EU member state, Russia and China make great play of supporting the territorial integrity and sovereignty of states and seem certain to block any attempt to overturn the resolution.

Additionally, the fact that Cyprus is a member of the EU makes the likelihood of recognition rather limited and potentially very costly in political terms. No other EU member would recognise the north. Even if there might be an inclination to do so in certain member states, there is no doubt that such a step would create massive political divisions within the European Union. In fact, the fallout in terms of European unity would be immeasurable. As for non-EU states, even if the EU decided not to enforce sanctions against a state for recognising the north, its relations with the EU would be hampered. It seems almost certain that the Cypriot government would try to block various agreements with the country. This could have very severe effects, especially on smaller or developing states. Of course, it is possible that some countries—perhaps some oil-rich Islamic states—might be willing to press ahead and establish formal diplomatic relations with the north. However, for the reasons just stated, the numbers willing to do so certainly wouldn't be large enough to give the TRNC any real legitimacy in international circles. It therefore seems highly unlikely that the recognition option presents an alternative to a negotiated solution.

IS FORMAL PARTITION A 'FAIR AND VIABLE' SOLUTION?

After almost fifty years of attempts to bridge the political divide between the two communities and almost forty years of efforts to broker reunification, many have questioned whether the time has come to accept defeat and accept the formal partition of the island. In some senses, it may seem like a logical solution given the reluctance of the two sides to reach a mutually acceptable settlement. However, such a move would run against established international thinking on managing ethnic conflicts. In numerous other cases (Bosnia and Iraq are two prominent examples), strenuous diplomatic efforts have been made to prevent states from breaking up. But as advocates of Kosovo's independence have argued, sometimes there is no viable option but to let a people within a state go their own way. Trying to force them back together would simply lead to further political instability and, possibly, bloodshed.

In terms of Cyprus specifically, arguments against division are mostly made on moral grounds. By accepting partition, the Greek Cypriots and the international community would effectively be legitimising a situation created through the use of force. Partition would effectively punish Greek Cypriots for the 1974 invasion, an act that has been recognised as contrary to international law. However, the moral question runs both ways. In the aftermath of the Annan Plan, many observers increasingly question whether the Turkish Cypriots should be forced to live in perpetual isolation and denied the right of self-determination because the Greek Cypriots insist on trying to leverage their international position to force the Turkish Cypriots to accept a secondary status in any new state.

Though there is much anger and bitterness within the Greek Cypriot community about the events of 1974, there is also a growing sense of pragmatism. In private, many Greek Cypriots have their doubts about efforts to reunite the island. In moderate circles, some appear to have concluded that the north is all but lost for good and that maybe it is time to open up discussions on a formal separation. Such an agreement would be based on the return of a certain proportion of territory to the Greek Cypriots (and compensation for properties not returned) in return for the Greek Cypriots' recognising the north and, ideally, allowing it to join the European Union. This type of land-for-peace deal would in many ways make sense, especially if linked to Turkish Cypriot accession to the EU.

Many Greek Cypriot nationalists appear to be reaching the same conclusion. Having come to terms with the fact that a bizonal, bicommunal federation is the only option available, and appalled with what this means in real terms, they realize that it might be better to keep the Republic of Cyprus as it is—a Greek Cypriot–controlled entity. While there is a certain degree of logic to this point of view, this argument seems unlikely to enter the mainstream of political debate anytime soon. No politician would want to be the first to come out with this view, even if it does reflect a far wider strand of thinking than outsiders generally realise. Therefore, while partition might represent a logical solution, at least from some perspectives, it seems likely that negotiations will continue to focus on reunification for the foreseeable future.

SUGGESTIONS FOR FURTHER READING

Asmussen, Jan. *Cyprus at War: Diplomacy and Conflict during the 1974 Crisis.* London: I. B. Tauris, 2008.

Attalides, Michael. *Cyprus: Nationalism and International Politics.* Mannheim, Germany: Bibliopolis, 2003.

Birand, Mehmet Ali. *Thirty Hot Days.* Nicosia, Cyprus: Rustem, 1985.

Brewin, Christopher. *The European Union and Cyprus.* Huntingdon, UK: Eothen Press, 2000.

Bryant, Rebecca. *Imagining the Modern: The Cultures of Nationalism in Cyprus.* London: I. B. Tauris, 2004.

Clerides, Glafcos. *Cyprus: My Deposition.* 4 vols. Nicosia, Cyprus: Alithea Press, n.d.

Constandinos, Andreas. *America, Britain, and the Cyprus Crisis of 1974: Calculated Conspiracy or Foreign Policy Failure?* London: AuthorHouse, 2009.

Crawshaw, Nancy. *Cyprus Revolt: Origins, Development, and Aftermath of an International Dispute.* London: Allen and Unwin, 1976.

Denktash, Rauf R. *The Cyprus Triangle.* London: Allen and Unwin, 1988.

Diez, Thomas, and Nathalie Tocci, eds. *Cyprus: A Conflict at the Crossroads.* Manchester, UK: Manchester University Press, 2009.

Dodd, Clement, ed. *The History and Politics of the Cyprus Conflict.* Palgrave Basingstoke, UK: Macmillan, 2010.

Durrell, Lawrence. *Bitter Lemons of Cyprus.* London: Faber and Faber, 2000.

Faustmann, Hubert, and Nicos Peristianis, eds. *Britain in Cyprus: Colonialism and Post-Colonialism, 1878–2006.* Mannheim, Germany: Bibliopolis, 2006.

Faustmann, Hubert, and Andrekos Varnava, eds. *Reunifying Cyprus: The Annan Plan and Beyond.* London: I. B. Tauris, 2009.

Foley, Charles. *Legacy of Strife: Cyprus from Rebellion to Civil War.* London: Penguin, 1964.

Hannay, David. *Cyprus: The Search for a Solution*. London: I. B. Tauris, 2005.

Hatzivassiliou, Evanthis. *The Cyprus Question, 1878–1960: The Constitutional Aspect*. Minneapolis: University of Minnesota, Minnesota Mediterranean and East European Monographs, 2002.

Henn, Francis. *A Business of Some Heat: The United Nations Force in Cyprus 1972–74*. Barnsley, UK: Pen and Sword Books, 2004.

Hitchens, Christopher. *Hostage to History: Cyprus from the Ottomans to Kissinger*. London: Verso, 1997.

Holland, Robert. *Britain and the Revolt in Cyprus, 1954–59*. Oxford, UK: Oxford University Press, 1998.

Joseph, Joseph S. *Cyprus: Ethnic Conflict and International Concern*. Basingstoke: UK: Macmillan, 1997.

Ker-Lindsay, James. *EU Accession and UN Peacemaking in Cyprus*. Basingstoke: UK: Palgrave Macmillan, 2005.

Ker-Lindsay, James, and Hubert Faustmann, eds. *The Government and Politics of Cyprus*. Bern, Switzerland, and Oxford, UK: Peter Lang, 2009.

Loizos, Peter. *The Heart Grown Bitter: A Chronicle of Cypriot War Refugees*. Cambridge, UK: Cambridge University Press, 1981.

Macris, Nicholas, ed. *The 1960 Treaties on Cyprus and Selected Subsequent Acts*. Mannheim, Germany: Bibliopolis, 2003.

Markides, Diana Weston. *Cyprus 1957–63: From Colonial Conflict to Constitutional Crisis. The Role of the Municipal Issue*. Minneapolis: University of Minnesota, Minnesota Mediterranean and East European Monographs, 2001.

Markides, Kyriacos C. *The Rise and Fall of the Cyprus Republic*. New Haven, CT: Yale University Press, 1977.

Mirbaheri, Farid. *Cyprus and International Peacemaking*. London: Hurst, 1998.

Morgan, Tabitha. *Sweet and Bitter Island: A History of the British in Cyprus*. London: I. B. Tauris, 2010.

Nicolet, Claude. *United States Policy towards Cyprus, 1954–1974: Removing the Greek-Turkish Bone of Contention*. Mannheim, Germany: Bibliopolis, 2001.

O'Malley, Brendan, and Ian Craig. *The Cyprus Conspiracy*. London: I. B. Tauris, 1999.

Palley, Claire. *An International Relations Debacle: The UN Secretary-General's Mission of Good Offices in Cyprus 1999–2004*. Oxford, UK: Hart Publishing, 2005.

Panteli, Stavros. *The Modern History of Cyprus*. London: Topline Publishing, 2005.

Papadakis, Yiannis. *Echoes from the Dead Zone: Across the Cyprus Divide*. London: I. B. Tauris, 2005.

Reddaway, John. *Burdened with Cyprus: The British Connection*. London: Weidenfeld and Nicolson, 1986.

Richmond, Oliver P. *Mediating in Cyprus: The Cypriot Communities and the United Nations*. London: Frank Cass, 1998.

Richmond, Oliver P., and James Ker-Lindsay, eds. *The Work of the UN in Cyprus. Promoting Peace and Development.* Basingstoke, UK: Palgrave Macmillan, 2001.

Salih, Halil Ibrahim. *Cyprus: The Impact of Diverse Nationalism on a State.* Tuscaloosa: University of Alabama Press, 1978.

Stephanides, Ioannis. *Isle of Discord: Nationalism, Imperialism, and the Making of the Cyprus Problem.* London: Hurst, 1999.

Tocci, Nathalie. *EU Accession Dynamics and Conflict Resolution: Catalysing Peace or Consolidating Partition in Cyprus.* Aldershot, UK: Ashgate, 2004.

Vassiliou, George. *From the President's Office: A Journey towards Reconciliation in a Divided Cyprus.* London: I. B. Tauris, 2010.

INDEX